THE POWER AND MEANING OF LOVE

Thomas Merton

THE POWER
AND MEANING
OF LOVE

SHELDON PRESS
LONDON

First published in Great Britain in 1976
by Sheldon Press, Marylebone Road, London NW1 4DU

This edition is a selection of essays from *Disputed Questions*
by Thomas Merton, by arrangement with the publishers
Farrar, Straus and Giroux, Inc., New York

Printed in Great Britain by
The Camelot Press Ltd, Southampton

ISBN 0 85969 063 6 cased
ISBN 0 85969 067 9 paper

THE AUTHOR

Thomas Merton was a monk of the Cistercian Order of Strict Observance. He was born in Prades, France, and spent his childhood in the United States, France and England. He attended Cambridge University in England and later Columbia University in America. After his conversion to Catholicism he entered the Abbey of Gethsemani where he wrote the vast majority of his prodigious output. Thomas Merton is the author of many books on spiritual, political and literary subjects; those published by Sheldon Press include *The Wisdom of the Desert*, *The Asian Journal*, *The Silent Life*, *Thomas Merton on Zen* and his autobiographical *The Seven Storey Mountain*. His growing interest in Eastern religions led him to attend a conference held in Bangkok in 1968 on the future of monastic life in Asia. He died while he was there.

CONTENTS

THE POWER AND MEANING OF LOVE

1 . *Love as a creative force—and its corruptions*

Man has lost Dante's vision of that "love which moves the sun and the other stars," and in so doing he has lost the power to find meaning in his world. Not that he has not been able to understand the physical world better. The disappearance of the simple medieval cosmogony upon which Dante built his structure of hell, purgatory, and heaven, has enabled man to break out of the limitations imposed upon his science by that ancient conception. And now he is prepared to fly out into those depths of space which terrified Pascal—and which continue to terrify anyone who is still human. Yet, though man has acquired the power to do almost anything, he has at the same time lost the ability to orient his life toward a spiritual goal by the things that he does. He has lost all conviction that he knows where he is going and what he is doing, unless he can manage to plunge into some collective delusion which promises happiness (sometime in the future) to those who will have learned to use the implements he has now discovered.

Man's unhappiness seems to have grown in proportion to his power over the exterior world. And anyone who claims to have a glib explanation of this fact had better take care that he too is not the victim of a delusion. For after all, this should not necessarily be so. God made man the ruler of the earth, and all science worthy of the name participates in some way in the wisdom and providence of the Creator. But the trouble is that unless the works of man's wisdom, knowledge and power participate in the merciful love of God, they are without real value for the world and for man. They do nothing to make man happy and they do not manifest in the world the glory of God.

Man's greatest dignity, his most essential and peculiar power, the most intimate secret of his humanity is his capacity to love. This power in the depths of man's soul stamps him in the image and likeness of God. Unlike other creatures in the world around us, we have access to the inmost sanctuary of our own being. We can enter into ourselves as into temples of freedom and of light. We can open the eyes of our heart and stand face to face with God our Father. We can speak to Him and hear Him answer. He tells us not merely that we are called to be men and to rule our earth, but that we have an even more exalted vocation than this. We are His sons. We are called to be godlike beings, and, more than that, we are in some sense called to be "gods." "Is it not written in the law, I said you are gods—and they are gods to whom the words of God are spoken?" (John 10:34-35; Ps. 81:6).

This vocation to be sons of God means that we must learn to love as God Himself loves. For God is love, and it is by loving as He loves that we become perfect as our heavenly Father is perfect (Matt. 5:48). Hence, while being called to govern and cultivate the world that God has given us, we are called at the same time to love everything and everyone in it. Nor is this love a matter of mere sentimental complacency. It has a dynamic spiritual meaning, for by this love we are called to redeem and transform the world in that same power which raised up Christ from the dead (Eph. 1:17-23). That power is the infinite love of the Father for His Son.

Love then is not only our own salvation and the key to the meaning of our own existence, but it is also the key to the meaning of the entire creation of God. It is true, after all, that our whole life is a participation in that cosmic liturgy of "the love which moves the sun and the other stars."

But what is love and how do we come to love as sons of God? Surely love is everywhere; man cannot live without it. If everybody loves, or tries to love, why is it that we are not made happy and redeemed by all this constant effort? The answer is that all that seems to be love is not so in reality.

The reality of love is judged, then, by its power to help man get beyond himself, to renew himself in transcending his present limitations. Though the function of natural love is to perpetuate man in time, the function of spiritual love is much greater still—to give man possession of eternity. This it does not merely by "saving man's soul" as an individual, but by establishing in time the eternal kingdom of God. The function of love is to build this spiritual kingdom of unity and peace, and to make man not only the exploiter of creation but truly its spiritual head and king.

A love that merely enables man to "enjoy himself," to remain at peace in a life of inert comfort and to bring into being replicas of himself is not to be regarded as true love. It does not represent a renewal, a progress, a step forward in building the kingdom of God.

True love leads a man to fulfilment, not by drawing things to himself but by forcing him to transcend himself and to become something greater than himself. True spiritual love takes the isolated individual, exacts from him labor, sacrifice, and the gift of himself. It demands that he "lose his life" in order to find it again on a higher level—in Christ.

All true love is a death and a resurrection in Christ. It has one imperious demand: that all individual members of Christ give themselves completely to one another and to the Church, lose themselves in the will of Christ and in the good of other men, in order to die to their own will and their own interests and "rise again" as other Christs. A love that does not tend to this transformation does not fulfil the exacting requirements of true spiritual love, and consequently lacks the power to develop and perpetuate man in his spirituality.

All true love is therefore closely associated with three fundamentally human strivings: with *creative work*, with *sacrifice*, and with *contemplation*. Where these three are present there is reliable evidence of spiritual life, at least in some inchoate form. There is reliable evidence of love. And the most important of the three is sacrifice.

Man's essential mystery is his vocation to be the son of God; but one of the deepest aspects of this mystery is precisely the fact that the fundamental temptation, the one to which Adam owes his fall, is the temptation to be "like unto God."

There is a singular necessity for man to be tried in that which is deepest and most essential about himself. And if we understand the meaning of this testing, we will understand the vital importance of love in the life of man. In the story of the fall of Adam, we see the tempter apparently suggesting that man attain to what he already possessed. *Eritis sicut dii*. But man was already "like unto God." For in the very act of creation God had said: "Let us make man to our image and likeness" (Gen. 1:26). Satan offered man what he already had, but he offered it with the appearance of something that he did not have. That is to say, he offered man the divine likeness as if it were *something more* than God had already given him, as if it were something that could be his apart from a gift of God, apart from the will of God, or even against the will of God.

Satan offered man the power to be like God *without loving Him*. And in this consisted what we call the "fall" and "original sin": that man elected to be "like unto a god" and indeed a god of his own, without loving God his Father and without seeking participation, by love, in the life and power and wisdom of God who is Love.

God wished man His son to be truly divine, to share in His own wisdom, power, providence, justice and kingship. And all this depended on one thing: the love by which alone man could participate in the divine life of his Father. Satan offered man a pseudo-divine life in a wisdom, knowledge, prudence, power, justice and kingship which had some reality in them, indeed, but which were only shadows and caricatures of the reality which is contained in and depends on God who is Love.

Love, then, is the bond between man and the deepest reality of his life. Without it man is isolated, alienated from himself, alienated from other men, separated from God, from truth, wisdom and strength. By love man enters into contact first with his own deepest self, then with his brother, who is his other self, and finally with the wisdom and power of God, the ultimate Reality. But love comes to man in the first place from God. Love is the gift which seals man's being with its fullness and its perfection. Love first makes man fully human, then gives him his divine stature, making him a son and a minister of God.

So necessary is love in the life of man that he cannot be altogether without it. But a love that does not seek reality only frustrates man in his inmost being, and this love that does not act as a bond between a man and reality is called sin. All sin is simply a perversion of that love which is the deepest necessity of man's being: a misdirection of love, a gravitation toward something that does not exist, a bond with unreality.

The difference between real and unreal love is not to be sought in the *intensity* of the love, or in its subjective *sincerity*, or in its *articulateness*. These three are very valuable qualities when they exist in a love that is real. But they are very dangerous when they are associated with a love that is fictitious. In neither case are they any sure indication of the nature of the love to which they belong, though it is true that one might expect man to feel an intense, sincere and articulate love only for a real object and not for an unreal one.

The trouble is that love is something quite other than the mere disposition of a subject confronted with an object. In fact, when love is a mere subject-object relationship, it is not real love at all. And therefore it matters little to inquire whether the object of one's love is real or not, since if our love is only our impulsion towards an "object" or a "thing," it is not yet fully love.

The reality of love is determined by the relationship itself which it establishes. Love is only possible between persons as persons. That is to say, if I love you, I must love you as a person and not as a thing. And in that case my relationship to you is not merely the relationship of a subject to an object, but it is analogous to my relationship to myself. It is, so to speak, a relationship of a subject to a subject. This strange-sounding expression is only another way of saying something very familiar: I must know how to love you *as myself*.

There might be a temptation, under the influence of modern philosophies, to misunderstand this subjective quality in love. It by no means signifies that one questions the real existence of the person loved, or that one doubts the reality of the relationship established with him by love. Such an illusion would indeed make Christian love impossible, or at best only a matter of fantasy. On the contrary, the subjectivity essential to love does not detract from objective reality but adds to it. Love brings us into a relationship with an objectively existing reality, but because it is love it is able to bridge the gap between subject and object and *commune in the subjectivity of the one loved*. Only love can effect this kind of union and give this kind of knowledge-by-identity with the beloved—and the concrete interiority and mystery of this knowledge of the beloved is not adequately described by the scholastic term "connaturality."

When we love another "as an object," we refuse, or fail, to pass over into the realm of his own spiritual reality, his personal identity. Our contact with him is inhibited by remoteness and by a kind of censorship which *excludes* his personality and uniqueness from our consideration. We are not interested in him as "himself" but only as another specimen of the human race.

To love another as an object is to love him as "a thing," as a commodity which can be used, exploited, enjoyed and then cast off. But to love another as a person we must begin by granting him his own autonomy and identity as a person. We have to love him for what he is in himself, and not for what he is to us. We have to love him for his own good, not for the good we get out of him. And this is impossible unless we are capable of a love which "transforms" us, so to speak, into the other person, making us able to see things as he sees them, love what he loves, experience the deeper realities of his own life as if they were our own. Without sacrifice, such a transformation is utterly impossible. But unless we are capable of this kind of transformation "into the other" while remaining ourselves, we are not yet capable of a fully human existence. Yet this capacity is the key to our divine sonship also. For it is above all in our relationship with God that love, considered as a subject-object relationship, is utterly out of the question.

It is true that we have to deal with God most of the time as if He were "an object," that is to say, confronting Him in concepts which present Him objectively to us. Yet, as everyone knows, we only really come to know God when we find Him "by love" hidden "within ourselves"—that is to say, "by connaturality." Yet, paradoxically, we cannot find God "within ourselves" unless we go "out of ourselves" by sacrifice. Only a sacrificial love which enables us to let go of ourselves completely and empty ourselves of our own will can enable us to find Christ in the place formerly occupied by our own selfhood. And in this sacrifice we cease, in a certain manner, to be the subject of an act of knowing and become the one we know by love.

When man acts according to the temptation of Satan to be "like unto God," he places himself as the *unique subject* in the midst of a world of objects. He alone is a "person," he alone feels, enjoys, thinks, wills, desires, commands. The manifestations of apparent thought, feeling, and desire on the part of others are of little or no concern to him, except insofar as they represent response to his own acts. He never "becomes" the other. On the contrary, the people around him are only objective manifestations of what goes on subjectively in himself. Hence his relationship with them is, if you like, a relationship with another self, yes, but only in the sense of an *added* self, a *supplementary* self, not in the sense of a different self. The selves of others are nothing except insofar as they are replicas of himself. And when this is carried to its logical extreme (as it is, for example, by the totalitarian dictator), then society at large is made over into the image of the leader. The individuals in such a society cease to have any purpose except that of reflecting and confirming the leader's megalomaniac idea of himself.

Man cannot live without love, and if the love is not genuine, then he must have some substitute—a corruption of real love. These corruptions are innumerable. Some of them are so obviously corrupt that they present no problem to the thinker. The only problem is that of avoiding them in actual behavior. Those which present a problem do so because they can seem, and claim to be, genuine love. These false forms of love base their claim on appeal to an ideal, and their falsity consists precisely in the fact that they tend to sacrifice persons to concepts. And since modern thought has deliberately renounced any effort to distinguish between what exists only in the mind and what exists outside the mind (dismissing the question as irrelevant), love has become more and more mental and abstract. It has become, in fact, a flight from reality and from that interpersonal relationship which constitutes its very essence.

This flight from the personal to the purely mental level

occurs in various ways, two of which can be taken as most typical of our time and of our society. One is what we might call a romantic or liberal approach to love; the other, a legalist or authoritarian approach.

What we call the romantic approach is that love of the good which sacrifices the persons and the values that are present and actual, to other values which are always out of reach. Here a shiftless individualism dignifies itself as the quest for an elusive ideal, whether in politics or art or religion or merely in one's relations with other men. Such love is apparently obsessed with "perfection." It passes from one object to another, examining it superficially, playing with it, tempting it, being tempted by it, and then letting go of it because it is not "the right object." Such love is therefore always discarding the real and actual in order to go on to something else, because the real and actual are never quite right, never good enough to be worthy of love.

Such love is really only an escape from love, because it refuses the obligation of entering into a real relationship which would render love at the same time possible and obligatory. Because it hates the idea of obligation, it cannot fully face even the possibility of such a relationship. Its romanticism is a justification of flight. It claims that it will only begin to love when it has found a worthy object— whether it be a person who can "really be loved," or an ideal that can really be believed in, or an experience of God that is definitive and binding.

In its liberal aspect, this love justifies itself by claiming to dispense everyone else from responsibility to love. It issues a general permission for all to practice the same irresponsibility under the guise of freedom. Romantic liberalism thus declares an open season on "perfect objects," and proceeds comfortably to neglect *persons* and realities which are present and actual, and which, in all their imperfection, still offer the challenge and the opportunity of genuine love.

One who attempts this romantic and liberal fight may entirely avoid commitment to any object, cause, or person; or he may, on the other hand, associate himself with other men in dedication to some social or private purpose. But when he does this his idealism tends to become either an excuse for inertia or a source of repeated demands upon his associates. Such demands are implicit accusations of their unworthiness, and invitations to become more worthy under threat of being rejected. The unworthy object is treated with long-suffering attempts at forgiveness and understanding; but each heroic effort in this direction makes the object more and more of an object. And such, indeed, is the purpose of "love" in this context.

One discovers, on investigation, that this liberal idealism is in fact a way of defending oneself against real involvement in an interpersonal relationship and of keeping other persons subdued and humiliated in the status of objects.

Communal life in this event becomes a shelter which, by providing an all-embracing cover of idealistic vagueness, enables us to take refuge from the present "thou" in the comforting generalizations of the less menacing "they."

The authoritarian and legalist corruption of love is also a refusal to love on the ground that the object is not worthy. But here, instead of undertaking a vast exploration in quest of the worthy object (which can never be found), the presence of the unworthy object becomes the excuse for a tyrannical campaign for worthiness, a campaign to which there is practically no end.

The legalist is perfectly convinced that he is right. In fact, he alone is right. Serene in his own subjectivity, he claims to make everyone else conform to his idea of what is right, obey his idea of the law, and carry out his policies. But since what is loved is the law or the state or the party or the policy, persons are treated as objects that exist in order to have the law enforced upon them, or to serve the state, or to carry out the policy.

Here the objectification of personality and of all spiritual values is carried to the extreme. Here is no longer any romantic compromise with personality as an ideal. Here what matters is the law and the state—or the dialectical process in history. To these the person must always be sacrificed, and there is no question of ever considering him as a person at all except hypothetically. Men are treated as objects who might be capable of being considered as persons if the law should ever come to be perfectly enforced, or if the state should come to be all powerful, or if society should come to be perfectly socialized.

The romantic and liberal error seeks the perfect person, the perfect cause, the perfect idea, the perfect experience. The authoritarian error seeks the perfect society, the perfect enforcement of its own law, in expectation of that perfect situation which will permit objects to turn into persons. Until then, love is a matter of enforcing the law, or stepping up production, and the kindest thing to all concerned is to exterminate everyone who stands in the way of the policy of the moment.

Two things are especially to be noticed when this authoritarian temper is pushed to its logical extreme and becomes totalitarian. Under a totalitarian regime, it is frankly considered more efficient to discount all individual and personal values and to reduce everyone to a condition of extreme objectivization. Whereas the romantic and liberal attitude is that personality should be reverenced at least in theory and as an ideal, here personality is regarded frankly as a danger, and its potentialities for free initiative are brutally discouraged. Not only is man treated as an object in himself, but he is reduced to servitude to material and economic processes, not for his own good but for the sake of "the state" or the "revolution."

This objectivization is justified, implicitly or explicitly, by doctrines which hold either that most races of men are in fact sub-human, or that man has not yet attained his human stature because of economic alienation. In either event, the question of right, of human dignity and other spiritual values of man is altogether denied any consideration.

For a Nazi to treat a Jew as a man, for a Communist to treat a counter-revolutionary as a human being would not only be a weakness but an unpardonable betrayal of the cause. This is all the more cogent when we realize that at any time, any faithful member of the party is liable without reason and without warning to be designated as a counter-revolutionary and thus forced outside the human pale, as something execrable beyond the power of word or thought. All this in order to pay homage to the collective myth. Such is the dignity and greatness of man when he has become "like unto a god."

In these two corruptions of love, error reaches out to affect everything this love attempts to accomplish. For a romantic, "sacrifice" is, in fact, a word which justifies the rejection of the other person as an "imperfect object" in order to pursue the search of an abstract ideal. "Contemplation" becomes a subjective day-dream concerned only with fantasies and abstractions and protected by the stern exclusion of all real claims upon our heart.

For an authoritarian, "sacrifice," "contemplation" and "work" all alike are expressed in ruthless enforcement of the law above all. Everyone, oneself as well as others, must be offered up on the altar of present policy. No other value counts, nothing else is worthy of a moment's concern.

We have seen how these two false forms of love operate in man's secular life. We shall consider, in detail, how they work in the life of the Christian.

II . *Love as a religious force—and its corruptions*

When Christ founded His Church and gave to men His "new commandment" that we should love one another as He has loved us, He made it clear that the Church could never be a mere aggregation of objects, or a collectivity made up of depersonalized individuals.

In all His dealings with men on earth, the Lord acted and spoke in such a way that He appealed always to the deepest and most inviolate recesses of each person. Even those who met Him in the most casual contacts, who cried out to Him from the roadside, asking His help, would be brought before Him and addressed directly, without hedging: "What dost *thou* ask? Canst *thou* believe?" Even a woman who secretly touched the hem of His garment when a thick crowd pressed against Him on all sides was called to speak to Him face to face. She had appealed to Him secretly, perhaps with an intention that had something in it half magical, regarding Him perhaps as a holy thing, a holy force, rather than as a person. But the power that He had felt go out from Him was the power of His love, the power that had been appealed to in His Person, and that demanded to be recognized in a dialogue of "Thou and I."

The Church is, in fact, the united Body of all those who have entered into this dialogue with Christ, those who have

been called by their name, or better still, by a new name
which no one knows but He who gave it and he who has
received it. It is the Body not only of those who know
Christ, who have heard of Him, or who have thought about
Him: it is the Body of those who know Him in all His mystical dimensions (Eph. 3:18) and who, in union with one
another and "all the saints," know the charity of Christ
which surpasses all understanding. It is the Body of those
who are "filled unto all the fullness of God" (Eph. 3:19).
For the Church is the *pleroma* of Christ, the "fullness of
Him who is filled all in all" (Eph. 2:23).

This mysterious expression of St. Paul points to the "sac-
rament" of the Church as the continuation of Christ's incarnation on earth, as a society which is more than any social organization, a spiritual and supernatural unity whose
members form one mystical Person, Christ the Lord.

Christ dwells in each one of His members just as truly as
He dwells in the whole Church, and that is why He is said
to be "all in all." Each one is, in a certain sense, Christ, insofar as Christ lives in him. And yet the whole Church is
one Christ.

Each member of the Church, however, "is Christ" only
insofar as he is able to transcend his own individual limitations and rise above himself to attain to the level of the
Christ-life which belongs to the entire Church. This mystery of plurality in unity is a mystery of love. For "in Christ"
we who are distinct individuals, with distinct characters,
backgrounds, races, countries, and even living in different
ages of the world, are all brought together and raised above
our limited selves in a unity of mystical love which makes us
"One"—"One Body and one Spirit. . . . One Lord, one
faith, one baptism, one God and Father of all who is above
all and through all and in us all" (Eph. 4:4-6). "For by

Christ we have access both in one Spirit to the Father"
(*ibid.*, 2:18). "That they all may be one as Thou Father in
Me and I in Thee, that they may be one in Us" (John
17:21).

Those who are one with Christ are also one with one another. But the New Testament shows us how intransigent
the Apostles were in demanding, without compromise, that
this unity be maintained on the highest and most personal
level. It is of course possible for a human being who is not
in the fullest sense a person to be a living and holy member
of the Church—as in the case of children who have not yet
attained the age of reason. But it is by no means the ideal of
the Church that her members should remain at this mental
and spiritual level all their lives. On the contrary, St. Paul
teaches that spiritual immaturity is equivalent to living on
the level of "carnal" men, which is a level of dissension and
division.

The unity of the Mystical Body depends on its members
attaining to maturity in Christ, that is to say, achieving the
full stature of spiritual manhood, of personality and responsibility and of freedom, in Christ Jesus (see 1 Cor. 1 and
2, Eph. 3:13 ff., etc). Failure to attain to this maturity
means inability to "receive the Spirit of Christ" or to "judge
the things of the Spirit." Consequently it means failure to
rise above the limitations of individuals or small groups, and
inability to meet others on a transcendent plane where all
are one in Christ while retaining their individual differences.

One who is not mature, not fully a person "in Christ,"
cannot understand the real nature of the mystery of Christ
as a union of many in one, because he is not yet able to live
on the level of Christ's love. Such love is foolishness to him,
though he may imagine he understands it. It remains a

closed book because he is still not fully a person and he is still not able to enter deeply into that dialogue of love in which he finds himself identified with his brother in the unanimity and love, the "we" which forms the Church, the Mystical Body of Christ.

Those of us today who seek to be Christians, and who have not yet risen to the level of full maturity in Christ, tend unfortunately to take one or other of the corrupt forms of love described above for the action of the Spirit of God and the love of Christ. It is this failure to attain to full maturity in love which keeps divisions alive in the world.

There is a "romantic" tendency in some Christians—a tendency which seeks Christ not in love of those flesh-and-blood brothers with whom we live and work, but in some as yet unrealized ideal of "brotherhood." It is always a romantic evasion to turn from the love of people to the love of love itself: to love mankind more than individual men, to love "brotherhood" and "unity" more than one's brothers, neighbors, and associates.

This corruption of love can be romantic also in its love of God. It is no longer Christ Himself that is loved and sought, but perhaps an objectivized "experience" of Christ, a degree of prayer, a mystical state. What is loved then ceases to be Christ, but the subjective reactions which are aroused in me by the supposed presence of Christ in thought or love or prayer.

The romantic tendency leads to a substitution of aestheticism, or false mysticism, or quietism, for genuine faith and love, and what it seeks in the Church is not so much reality as a protection against responsibility. Failing to establish a true dialogue with our brother in Christ, this fallacy thwarts all efforts at real unity and cooperation among Christians.

It is not necessary to point out that the danger of substi-

tuting legalism for Christian love also exists. This danger is
perhaps even more actual than that of the romantic error,
and tends to become increasingly so in a totalitarian age.
Fortunately, the terrible excesses of totalitarian authoritarianism are there to stimulate in us a healthy reaction and a
return to the liberty of the sons of God.

The Church must have her structure of law and discipline,
like any other visible society of men on earth. In heaven
there will be no Law for the elect but God Himself, who is
Charity. In heaven, obedience will be entirely swallowed
up in love. On earth, unfortunately, not all are able to live
without a Law, though as St. Paul says, there should in reality be no need of a Law for the saints. Not all are able to
rise to that level of love which, in all things, is a fulfilment
of the Law and therefore needs no Law (Gal. 5:13-23).

It is therefore not "legalism" to insist that we must all fulfil the duties of our state and of our proper vocations with
all fidelity and in a spirit of humble obedience. There exists
in the Church a juridical authority, a hierarchy of ministers
through whom the Holy Spirit manifests the will of God in
an easily recognizable way. To reject this authority and still
claim to love God and the unity of His Church would be a
manifest illusion. It has not infrequently happened in the
past that some who have believed themselves inspired by
charity have in fact rejected obedience and thus done much
to dismember the unity of the Body of Christ.

Nothing could be more tragic than a pseudo-mystical enthusiasm which mistakes strong emotion for the voice of
God, and on the basis of such emotion claims a "spiritual"
authority to break away from communion with the rest of
the faithful and to despise legitimate authority. This is not
that strong sacrificial love of God which rises above in-

dividual interests and cements divergent groups in a transcendent unity. Such errors savor of the romanticism we
have discussed above.

Legalism, on the other hand, is another weak form of love
which in the end produces dissension, destroys communion,
and for all its talk about unity, tends by its narrowness and
rigidity to create divisions among men. For legalism, refus-
ing to see truth in anybody else's viewpoint, and rejecting
human values *a priori* in favor of the abstract letter of the
law, is utterly incapable of "rising above" its own limitations
and meeting another on a superior level. Hence the legalistic Christian (like the legalistic Jew who caused so much
trouble to St. Paul), instead of broadening his view to comprehend the views of another, insists on bringing everyone
else into the stifling confines of his own narrowness.

Legalism is not synonymous with conservatism or tradi-
tionalism. It can equally well be found in those social-
minded Christians who, by their contact with Communism
in the movement for social justice, have unwittingly contracted a spirit of totalitarian narrowness and intolerance.
The temptation to legalism arises precisely when the apparent holiness of a *cause* and even its manifest rightness blinds
us to the holiness of individuals and persons. We tend to
forget that charity comes first and is the only Christian
"cause" that has the right to precedence over every other.

Legalism in practice makes law and discipline more important than love itself. For the legalist, law is more worthy
of love than the persons for whose benefit the law was insti-
tuted. Discipline is more important than the good of souls
to whom discipline is given, not as an end in itself but as a
means to their growth in Christ.

The authoritarian Christian does not love his brother so
much as he loves the cause or the policy which he wants

his brother to follow. For him, love of the brother consists, not in helping his brother to grow and mature in love as an individual person loved by Christ, but in making him "toe the line" and fulfil exterior obligations, without any regard for the interior need of his soul for love, understanding and communion. All too often, for the legalist, love of his brother means punishing his brother, in order to force him to become "what he ought to be." Then, when this is achieved, perhaps the brother can be loved. But until then he is not really "worthy of love."

This is in reality a fatal perversion of the Christian spirit. Such "love" is the enemy of the Cross of Christ because it flatly contradicts the teaching and the mercy of Christ. It treats man as if he were made for the sabbath. It loves concepts and despises persons. It is the kind of love that says *corban* (see Mark 7:9-13) and makes void the commandment of God "in order to keep the traditions of men" (*ibid.*).

The reason why this legalism is a danger is precisely because it can easily be a perversion of true obedience as well as a perversion of love. Authoritarianism has a way of becoming so obsessed with the *concept* of obedience that it ends by disobeying the will of God and of the Church in all that is most dear to the Heart of Christ. It is the obedience of the son who says, "Yes, I go" and afterwards does not go to carry out the command of his father. The obsession with law and obedience as *concepts* and *abstractions* ends by reducing the love of God, and of God's will, to a purely arbitrary fiction.

"Obedience" and "discipline" alone cannot guarantee the unity of the Body of Christ. A living organism cannot be held together by merely mechanical and exterior means. It must be unified by its own interior life-principle. The life of the Church is divine Love itself, the Holy Spirit. Obedience and discipline are necessary to prevent us from separating ourselves, unconsciously, from the guidance of the Invisible Spirit. But merely bringing people to submit to authority by external compulsion is not sufficient to unite them in a vital union of love with Christ in His Church. Obedience without love produces only dead works, external conformity, not interior communion.

Doubtless there are very few Christians who, in actual fact, carry this legalism to a dangerous or scandalous extreme. But there remains a taint of legalism in the spirituality of a great many modern Christians, especially among religious. It is so easy to satisfy oneself with external conformity to precepts instead of living the full and integral life of charity which religious rules are intended to promote.

Here the danger is not one of a malicious and definitive perversion of the Christian spirit, but rather of spiritual immaturity. But the danger of this immaturity must nevertheless not be despised, for, as we have said, it frustrates the spontaneous and fruitful growth of charity in individuals, in religious communities and in the Church herself.

A sincere and invincible ignorance may often be the cause of a great deal of this immaturity: the ignorance of those who lead their Christian lives according to superficial formulas that are poorly understood.

For a great many religious of the present day, "love" and "obedience" are so perfectly equated with one another that they become identical. Love is obedience and obedience is love. In practice, this means that love is cancelled out and all that remains is obedience—plus a "pure intention" which by juridical magic transforms it into "love."

The identification of obedience with love proceeds from a

superficial understanding of such dicta as: "Love is a union of wills," "Love seeks to do the will of the beloved." These sayings are all very true. But they become untrue when in practice our love becomes the love of an abstract "will," of a juridical decree, rather than the love of a Person—and of the persons in whom He dwells by His Spirit!

A distinction will be useful here. To say that love (whether it be the love of men or the love of God) is a union of wills, does not mean that a mere external *conformity* of wills is love. The conformity of two wills brought into line with each other through the medium of an external regulation may perhaps clear the way for love, but it is not yet love. Love is not a mere mathematical equation or abstract syllogism. Even with the best and most sincere of intentions, exterior conformity with a regulation cannot be made, by itself, to constitute a union of wills in love. Why? Because unless "union of wills" means something concrete, a union of hearts, a union of spirits, *a communion between persons*, it is not a real enough union to constitute love.

A communion between persons implies interiority and depth. It involves the whole being of each person—the mind, the heart, the feelings, the deepest aspiration of the spirit itself. Such union manifestly excludes revolt, and deliberate mutual rejection. But it also presupposes individual differences—it safeguards the autonomy and character of each as an inviolate and solitary person. It even respects the inevitable ambivalences found in the purest of friendships. And when we observe the real nature of such communion, we see that it can really never be brought about merely by discipline and submission to authority.

The realm of obedience and of regulation, however great its value, however crucial its importance, is something so entirely different that it does little to effect this personal communion one way or the other. It merely removes external obstacles to this communion. But the communion itself implies much more than mere submission or agreement to some practical imperative. Communion means mutual understanding, mutual acceptance, not only in exterior acts to be carried out, but in regard to the inviolate interiority and subjectivity of those who commune with one another. Love not only accepts what the beloved desires, but, above all, it pays the homage of its deepest interior assent to what he *is*. From this everything else follows, for, as we know, the Christian is *Christ*.

Hence, as the Gospel teaches us (Matt. 25:31-46), a Christian loves not simply by carrying out commands issued by Christ, in heaven, in regard to this "object" which happens to be a fellow Christian. The Christian loves his brother because the brother "is Christ." He seeks the mind of the Church because the Church "is Christ." He unites himself in the worship of the Church because it is the worship which Christ offers to His Father. His whole life is lived in the climate of warmth and energy and love and fruitfulness which prevades the whole Church and every member of the Church, because the Church is a Body filled with its own life—filled with the Spirit of Christ.

A good example of the true climate of Christian obedience, a climate most favorable to the growth of love, is found in the Rule of St. Benedict. Benedict of Nursia is not only a lawgiver. More important still is the fact that he is a loving Father. The Rule opens with a characteristically Christian invitation to a dialogue of love between persons, and it is this dialogue which, on every page, elevates Benedictine obedience to the level of charity.

Love is the motive for monastic obedience, not love as

an abstract and lifeless "intention," but love flourishing in a warm and concrete contact of persons who know, who understand, and who revere one another. Here obedience is not for the sake of the law but for the sake of Christ. It is not just "supernaturalized" in the sense of being mentally "offered up." It is totally transfigured by a faith which sees that Christ lives and acts in the *personal relationship,* the mutual respect and love, which form the bond between the spiritual father and his spiritual son. Each, in fact, reveres Christ in the other. Each realizes that what matters is not the exact carrying out of an abstract and formal decree that has no concern for individual cases, but that the important thing is this relationship, which is a union in the Holy Spirit. It is for the sake of this sabbath of monastic peace that the Rule is written. And the sabbath itself exists for the men who keep the Rule.

Christ came not to destroy the Law. But neither did He come merely to *enforce* it. He came to *fulfil* the Law. Everyone knows that this "fulfilment" by Christ means more than that He simply carried out the Law in a way that would not have been possible for everyone else. That, of course, is part of the meaning. Christ satisfied all the exigencies of the Law by "blotting out the handwriting of the decree (the Law) which was contrary to us. And He hath taken the same out of the way, fastening it to the Cross" (Col. 2:14). But more than that, He Himself, in His very Person, is the fulfilment of the Law. That is to say, Christ in us, Christ in His Church, dwelling in the world in the unity of charity that makes men one in Him: this is the fulfilment of the Law.

The community of the primitive Church after Pentecost, in which all the believers were of one heart and of one soul —this was Christ on earth, and the fulfilment of the Law.

To attempt to satisfy the exigencies of the Law by a quantity of ritual acts and multiple observances, to abide by the countless regulations and decrees of the Torah, this was a futile and hopeless task, rendered all the more ridiculous by the fact that Christ had already "emptied" all these things of their content by dying on the Cross and rising from the dead. Indeed, to return to all these practices was to return to servitude under the "elements of this world," and St. Paul rightly became angry with his "senseless Galatians" who had been "bewitched so that they *should not obey the truth*" (Gal. 3:1).

Obsession with the works of the Law is, then, disobedience to the truth, and a practical contempt for the Cross of Christ (*ibid.*). Obviously the Christian has to be rich in good works, must bring forth fruit. But how does he bring forth fruit? By "remaining in Christ and in the love of Christ" (John 15:1-8). The community of the Church and the life of the Church is then Christ in the world, and the acts of that community are the acts of Christ.

The Christian who no longer has to worry about servitude to the works of the Law need have but one concern: to remain in the community of the faithful, to remain in that love and warmth and spiritual light which pervade the holy society of the Church, to unite himself in simplicity with the holy yet ordinary lives of his brethren, their faith, their worship and their love—this is all. For to live thus, united with the brethren by love, is to live in Christ who has fulfilled the Law. "They were persevering in the doctrine of the apostles and in the communication of the breaking of bread and in prayers . . . and all that were believers were together and had all things in common. Their possessions and goods they sold and divided them to all according as

every one had need. And continuing daily with one accord
in the temple and breaking bread from house to house,
they took their meat with gladness and simplicity of heart,
praising God and having favor with all the people" (Acts
2:42-47).

Christ commanded His disciples to love one another, and
this commandment summed up all of His will and contained everything else necessary for salvation.

This was not, however, intended to be another commandment of the same kind as the Decalogue—something
difficult to be done, a duty to be performed in order to
satisfy the demands of God. This is an entirely different
kind of commandment. It is like the commandment by
which God says, "Let there be light," or says to man, "Stand
up, live, be My son." It is not a demand for this or that
work, it is a word of life, a creative word, making man into a
new being, making his society into a new creation.

The command to love creates a new world in Christ. To
obey that command is not merely to carry out a routine
duty; it is to enter into life and to continue in life. To love
is not merely righteousness, it is transformation from brightness to brightness as by the Spirit of the Lord.

Here, of course, love and obedience are inseparable,
not in the sense that obedience is coextensive with love, but
in the sense that he who loves fulfills all the commands of
the law by loving. To obey is not necessarily to love, but to
love is necessarily to obey.

Why does God desire this love from men? Because by it
His mercy and His glory are manifested in the world,
through the unity of the faithful in Christ. God desires the
unity of the Church in order that "men may see what is
the dispensation of the mystery which hath been hidden

from eternity in God who created all things. That the mani-
fold wisdom of God may be made known to the principali-
ties and powers in the heavenly places through the Church"
(Eph. 3:9-10).

Love is the key to the meaning of life. It is at the same
time transformation in Christ and the discovery of Christ.
As we grow in love and in unity with those who are loved by
Christ (that is to say, all men), we become more and more
capable of apprehending and obscurely grasping something
of the tremendous reality of Christ in the world, Christ in
ourselves, and Christ in our fellow man.

The transcendent work of Christian love is also at every
moment a work of faith: not only faith in dogmas proposed
to our obedient minds by holy Church, not only faith in abstract propositions, but faith in the present reality of Christ,
faith in the living dialogue between our soul and Christ,
faith in the Church of Christ as the one great and central
reality which gives meaning to the cosmos.

But what does this faith imply? Here again the familiar
phrase "seeing Christ in my brother" is subject to a sadly
superficial interpretation. How many Christians there are,
especially priests and religious, who do not hesitate to assert
that this involves a sort of mental sleight-of-hand, by which
we deftly do away with our neighbor in all his concreteness,
his individuality, his personality with its gifts and limitations, and replace him by a vague and abstract presence of
Christ.

Are we not able to see that by this pitiful subterfuge we
end up by trying to love, not Christ in our brother, but
Christ *instead* of our brother? It is this, in fact, which explains the painful coldness and incapacity for love that are

sometimes found in groups of men or women most earnestly "striving for perfection." It also accounts for so many avoidable failures in the apostolate on the part of those who are so sincere, so zealous, and yet frighten people away from Christ by the frozen rigidity and artificiality of their lives.

Our charity is intended to give glory to God, not by enabling us to multiply meritorious acts on an imaginary "account" recorded for us in a heavenly bank, but by enabling us to see Christ and find Him where He is to be found, in our brother and in the Church.

The purpose of charity is not only to unite us to God in secret but also to enable God to show Himself to us openly. For this we have to resolutely put away our attachment to natural appearance and our habit of judging according to the outward face of things. I must learn that my fellow man, just as he is, whether he is my friend or my enemy, my brother or a stranger from the other side of the world, whether he be wise or foolish, no matter what may be his limitations, "*is Christ.*" No qualification is needed about whether or not he may be in the state of grace. Jesus in the parable of the sheep and the goats did not stop to qualify, or say: "Whenever you did it to one of these My least brethren, *if he was in the state of grace,* you did it to Me." Any prisoner, any starving man, any sick or dying man, any sinner, any man whatever, is to be regarded as Christ—this is the formal command of the Savior Himself.

This doctrine is far too simple to satisfy many modern Christians, and undoubtedly many will remain very uneasy with it, tormented by the difficulty that perhaps, after all, this particular neighbor is a bad man and is foredoomed to hell, and therefore cannot be Christ. The solution of this difficulty is to unite oneself with the Spirit of Christ, to start thinking and loving as a Christian, and to stop being a hair-splitting pharisee.

Our faith is not supposed to be a kind of radio-electric eye which is meant to assess the state of our neighbor's conscience. It is the needle by which we draw the thread of charity through our neighbor's soul and our own soul and sew ourselves together in one Christ. Our faith is given us not to see *whether or not* our neighbor is Christ, but to recognize Christ in him and to help our love make both him and ourselves more fully Christ.

One of the themes that has constantly recurred throughout this article is that corrupt forms of love wait for the neighbor to "become a worthy object of love" before actually loving him. This is not the way of Christ. Since Christ Himself loved us when we were by no means worthy of love and still loves us with all our unworthiness, our job is to love others without stopping to inquire whether or not they are worthy. That is not our business and, in fact, it is nobody's business. What we are asked to do is to love; and this love itself will render both ourselves and our neighbor worthy if anything can.

Indeed, that is one of the most significant things about the power of love. There is no way under the sun to make a man worthy of love except by loving him. As soon as he realizes himself loved—if he is not so weak that he can no longer bear to be loved—he will feel himself instantly becoming worthy of love. He will respond by drawing a mysterious spiritual value out of his own depths, a new identity called into being by the love that is addressed to him.

Needless to say, only genuine love can draw forth such a response, and if our love fails to do this, perhaps it is because it is corrupted with unconscious romanticism or legalism and, instead of loving the brother, is only manipulating and exploiting him in order to make him fit in with our own hidden selfishness.

If I allow the Holy Spirit to work in me, if I allow Christ to use my heart in order to love my brother with it, I will soon find that Christ loving in me and through me has brought to light Christ in my brother. And I will find that the love of Christ in my brother, loving me in return, has drawn forth the image and the reality of Christ in my own soul.

This, then, is the mystery of Christ manifesting Himself in the love which no longer regards my brother as an object or as a thing, which no longer treats him merely as a friend or an associate, but sees in him the same Lord who is the life of my own soul. Here we have a communion in a subjectivity that transcends every object of knowledge, because it is not just the climate of our own inner being, the peculiar silence of our own narrow self, but is at once the climate of God and the climate of all men. Once we know this, then, we can breathe the sweet air of Christ, a divine air, which is the breath of Christ.

This "air" is God Himself—the Holy Spirit.

A RENAISSANCE HERMIT: BL. PAUL GIUSTINIANI

Just as the Church of God can never be without martyrs, so too she can never be without solitaries, for the hermit, like the martyr, is the most eloquent witness of the Risen Christ. It was on the night of Easter that the Risen Savior breathed upon His Apostles, that they might receive of His Spirit, Who had not been given before because Christ was not yet glorified. St. Paul has told us that all who are sons of God are activated and moved by the Spirit of God. They have the Spirit of Christ because they belong to Christ. Having His Spirit, they live no longer according to the flesh but according to the Spirit. *Qui vero secundum Spiritum sunt, quae sunt Spiritus sentiunt.*[1] Therefore they are of one mind and one Spirit with Jesus Christ.

Now at the beginning of His public life, Jesus was led into the desert by the Spirit, that He might engage in single

[1] Romans 8:5.

combat with the devil. The struggle in the desert was the
prelude to the struggle in the Garden of the Agony. This
last was the exemplar and meritorious cause of the charity of
all the martyrs and all the hermits who would be tested, like
Christ Himself, in the furnace of tribulation because they
were pleasing to God. The Church of God, triumphing in
her martyrs and ascetics, would thus be able to declare with
Christ Himself: "The prince of this world indeed comes,
and he has no part in me: but he comes that the world
may know that I love the Father!" [2]

There must, therefore, be hermits. Nor is this only because there will always be men who desire solitude. The
Christian hermit is one who is led into the desert by the
Spirit, not by the flesh, even though he may well have a
natural inclination to live alone. Our own time has seen
hermits like the Dominican, Père Vayssière, who entered
the Order of Preachers knowing that he wanted to preach
the Gospel, and completely unaware that he would spend
most of his life in solitude at La Sainte Baume. Nor must
there always be hermits merely because there are always contemplative souls, or because the contemplative naturally
seeks physical solitude: (For without the efficacious desire of
exterior solitude, interior solitude will always remain a fantasy or an illusion.) The true reason for the persistence of
hermits even in ages which are most hostile to the solitary
ideal is that the exigencies of Christian life *demand* that
there be hermits. The Kingdom of God would be incomplete without them, for they are the men who seek God
alone with the most absolute and undaunted and uncompromising singleness of heart. If we have forgotten that the
Fathers of the Church assigned to the hermit a high, even
the highest place among all Christian vocations, a modern

[2] John, 14:30-31.

theologian, Dom Anselm Stolz, is there to remind us of the fact.[3] And now another Benedictine, Dom Jean Leclercq, has added an important volume to the slowly growing collection of works on the solitary life appearing in our own time.[4]

This book is all the more important because it introduces us to a hermit as interesting as he is unknown—a surprising figure, rising up almost unaccountably in the Italy of Raphael and Macchiavelli, Castiglione and Michelangelo Buonarotti. Paul Giustiniani became a novice at Camaldoli in 1510. That is to say that he entered the most ancient of the eremitical Orders that have survived in the Western Church. Camaldoli goes back to the tenth century and Saint Romuald. Less famous than the Chartreuse, Camaldoli nevertheless has retained more of the aspect of an ancient "laura" than we would find in any Charterhouse. The Camaldolese idea is simply to apply the Rule of St. Benedict to the eremitical life. St. Benedict declared, of course, that his Rule was written for cenobites. Therefore, the Camaldolese idea presupposes, first of all, a *cenobium*, a monastery where the monks live and work and pray in community. But St. Benedict also holds the solitary life in high honor, and suggests that certain monks, after a long probation in the monastery, may be called by God to a hermitage. St. Romuald made it possible for monks to have solitude without losing anything of the *bonum obedientiae* which is the treasure of monastic life, and without departing from that life in common, the life of fraternal charity, which is the security of all who do not feel themselves equal to the hero-

---

[3] Dom A. Stolz, O.S.B. *L'Ascèse Chrétienne*, Chevetogne, 1948, c. 1.
[4] *La Vie Erémitique d'après la Doctrine du Bienheureux. Paul Giustiniani*, Paris, 1955. (The present essay was written as a preface to this book by Dom Leclercq.)

ism of another Anthony. The *Sacro Eremo* of Camaldoli is therefore a community of hermits, a village of ancient cells hidden in a pine forest several thousand feet above sea level in the Appenines behind Arrezzo.

Paul Giustiniani entered Camaldoli at a time when the eremitical fervor had lost some of its ancient heat, and he left it for a stricter solitude. Eventually he was to start a new eremitical congregation of his own, the Hermits of Monte Corona, who still have a community at Frascati outside Rome and several others in Italy, Spain, and Poland. News has even been received of a recent foundation in the United States, in Ohio. Giustiniani bears the same relation to Camaldoli as the Abbé de Rancé does to the Order of Citeaux, and, in another sense, as Dom Innocent Lemasson does to the Chartreuse. Like each of these great men, Paul Giustiniani seeks to rekindle the ancient fire that is burning low in an age that has no love for asceticism, for contemplation or for solitude. It is therefore the greatest interest to have at our disposal a volume that brings together from his various works, most of which are inaccessible, a complete doctrine of the solitary life.

Let us now turn to the doctrine of Blessed Paul, whose name recalls to our minds the half legendary figure of the "first hermit" whom St. Anthony is supposed to have discovered in a cave where he had lived for over a hundred years unknown to men.

The eremitical life is above all solitary. St. Romuald chose to settle in the once inviolable forests of Camaldoli and to seek God in a solitude that was *sacred*, that is to say entirely consecrated to Him. The inviolable character of "holy solitude" is a witness to the infinite transcendence of Him Whose holiness elevates Him above all things. In order to seek Him Who is inaccessible the hermit himself becomes inaccessible. But within the little village of cells centered about the Church of the *Eremo* is a yet more perfect solitude: that of each hermit's own cell. Within the cell is the hermit himself, in the solitude of his own soul. But—and this is the ultimate test of solitude—the hermit is not alone with himself: for that would not be a sacred loneliness. Holiness is life. Holy solitude is nourished with the Bread of Life and drinks deep at the very Fountain of all Life. The solitude of a soul enclosed within itself is death. And so the authentic, the really sacred solitude is the infinite solitude of God Himself, Alone, in Whom the hermits are alone.

From this obligation to seek interior solitude flow all the other demands made upon the hermit, the other essential obligations of his state: silence, stability, recollection, mortification, labor, fasting, vigils and prayer. These detach the soul from all that is not God. They are not peculiar to the hermit. They belong to the monastic life wherever it is found. But the hermit has a very special obligation to practice them, without however departing from discretion which is one of the most important virtues of the solitary. After all, it is discretion which teaches us to live by the interior guidance of the Holy Spirit. It is discretion which teaches us to distinguish between the voice of the Spirit and the voice of the flesh or of the evil one. Discretion does not permit us to be cowards, but neither does it allow us to fall headlong into the abyss of vanity, pride, or presumption. Without discretion, the solitary life ends fatally in disaster.

In the true spirit of St. Benedict, Paul Giustiniani declares that even in the hermitage the best mortifications are those which are not of our own choice, and that even the hermit should seek to please God more by great fidelity in his ordinary duties than by extraordinary feats of ascetic heroism. The life of the solitary will be a continual warfare, in which the flesh fights not only against the spirit but against the flesh itself and in which the spirit also fights not only against the flesh but even against the spirit.

It is here, in this inexpressible rending of his own poverty, that the hermit enters, like Christ, into the arena where he wages the combat that can never be told to anyone. This is the battle that is seen by no one except God, and whose vicissitudes are so terrible that when victory comes at last, the total poverty and emptiness of the victor are so absolute that there is no longer any place in his heart for pride.

Such is the *eremitica puritas* which opens the way for contemplation. Without this "annihilation" the solitary might perhaps be tempted to seek rest in the consolations of God for their own sake. He might enjoy a selfish and self-complacent solitude in which he was delivered from responsibilities and inundated with supernatural favors. In words that remind us of St. John of the Cross, Paul Giustiniani speaks of the false contemplatives who "are displeased by everything that deprives them of the rest they think they have found in God but which they seek, really, in themselves. Their only care is to seek after peace, not in things below them, not in themselves, but in God; however they desire this peace not for the glory of God, but out of love for themselves."

Nor does the sacredness of solitude and the true eremitical purity allow the hermit to become absorbed in a zeal that does not extend beyond the welfare or reputation of his own monastery and his own Order, still less beyond his own progress and his own virtues. A life alone with God is something too vast to include such limited objectives within its range. It reaches up to God Himself, and in doing so embraces the whole Church of God.

Meanwhile the hermit supports this interior poverty of

spirit with the greatest exterior poverty. He must live like the poorest of the poor, *Eremitica puritas* is the peace of one who is content with bare necessities. Such peace is impossible where poverty is a mere matter of exterior form. The hermit is not one who, though deprived of the right to possess them, actually has the use of better objects and enjoys more plentiful comforts than could ever be afforded by the materially poor. The eremitical community itself must be a poor community. And although this simplicity guarantees the hermit a high place in the Church, he himself will remember that his elevation is in reality a matter of humility and abjection. He takes no part in the active affairs of the Church because he is too poor to merit a place in them. For him to accept prelacy would be an infidelity because it would be an act of presumption. Paul Giustiniani pursues this subject of poverty into the most remote corners of the hermit's soul. The solitary will not even pride himself on his strict observances, or compare himself with religious of other Orders. He will avoid the supreme folly of those who, having nothing in the world but their humility, lose even that by boasting of it! By this perfect forgetfulness of himself, the hermit merits to be called the successor of the martyrs.

There is a positive side to all this. Solitude is not sought for its own sake. If the eremitical life is the highest form of Christianity it is because the hermit aspires more than anyone else to perfect union with Christ. Jesus Himself is the living Rule of the hermit, just as He is the model of every religious. It is Christ Himself who calls us into solitude, exacting of us a clean break with the world and with our past, just as He did of St. Anthony. Perhaps more than any other the solitary life demands the presence of the Man Christ Who lives and suffers in us. Even if we worshipped the one true God in the desert, without the Incarnate Word our soli-

tude would be less than human, and therefore far short of
the divine: without Him no one comes to the Father. Without Jesus we all too easily fulfil the words of Pascal—"qui
veut faire l'ange, fait la bête." Solitude must therefore trans-
late itself into the three words: "Cum Christo Vivere"—to
live with Christ. Solitude is a fortress that protects the heart
against all that is not Christ, and its only function is to allow Christ to live in us. Solitude spiritualizes the whole man,
transforms him, body and soul, from a carnal to a spiritual
being. It can only do so in the Spirit of Christ Who elevates
our whole being in God, and does not divide man's personality against itself like those false asceticisms which St. Paul
knew to be enemies of the Cross of Christ.

In a hymn to this solitude which is "too unknown," Giustiniani says: "It is thou that announcest the coming of the
Holy Spirit: and not only announcest Him, but bringest
Him into the human heart just as the dawn, which an-
nounces the day, brings to our eyes the brightness of the
sun."

This brings us to the mystical doctrine of Paul Giustiniani
who, like the Fathers of the Church, believed that the eremitical life was ordered exclusively to contemplation and was
the only purely contemplative life. Like the Fathers, also,
when he speaks of contemplation he means mystical contemplation. This is without doubt the most interesting and
important part of the book. In pages that remind us now of
St. Catherine of Genoa, now of St. Bernard, now even of
John Ruysbroeck, Paul Giustiniani teaches us a doctrine
elevated but sure since his whole emphasis is on the coin-
cidence of humility and greatness in the experience of
union. The way of contemplation is never exalted, and the
hermit must aspire to be "lifted up" in no other way than
on the Cross, with Christ. He does not reach the Father ex-

cept through the abjection of Christ, Who lives again in the hermit that *exinanivit semetipsum* by which He merited for us a share in His sonship and in His divine glory. Reading the pages of Giustiniani on annihilation we are reminded of St. John of the Cross, who describes the soul that is purified and ready for union with God in these terms:

"In this detachment the spiritual soul finds its quiet and repose; for, since it covets nothing, nothing wearies it when it is lifted up, and nothing oppresses it when it is cast down, for it is in the center of its humility; since, when it covets anything, at that very moment it becomes wearied." [5]

The whole purpose of the solitary life is to bring the soul into the "center of her humility" and to keep it there. The hermit does not pretend to have acquired any esoteric secret or any exalted technique by which he penetrates into the mystery of God. His only secret is the humility and poverty of Christ and the knowledge that God lifts up those who have fallen: *Dominus erigit elisos*. Without this humility, the contemplatives can be a prey to "all the illusions." For "the true servants of Christ love God with all their being, and do not love themselves at all. They keep themselves so perfectly under the guardianship of humility as to be known by God alone, but unknown to men."

But once he is perfectly united with the poverty and humility of Christ crucified, the solitary lives entirely by the life and Spirit of Christ. He can therefore be transformed and elevated to the perfection of selfless love for God, that love in which he no longer knows himself or anything else, but only God alone. This is the culmination of mystical love in which the contemplative "loves God in God." It is here that we detect interesting resonances from the doctrine of

[5] Ascent of Mt. Carmel—Vol. I, ch. 1, #13, p. 63 (Complete Works of Saint John of the Cross; Newman Press, 1949).

Ruysbroeck. Whether or not Giustiniani knew the Flemish
mystic, a comparison between them might be interesting.
This is not the place for it. What is more important here is
to notice that this love for God in God, which is the highest
perfection of the solitary and contemplative life is also the
perfect justification of the hermit's utility to the rest of the
Church.

The hermit is not to be considered a "dynamo" of apostolic power in the crude sense of a machine actively producing a great quantity of prayers and works of penance for the
salvation of souls. We have seen that quantity becomes a
negligible factor in the life of *eremitica puritas*. The solitary
should not seek to replace his lost possessions by merely nu-
merical accumulation of prayers and good works over which
he can gloat like a happy miser at the end of each day. In
praying to God for souls, he realizes it is not so important to
know the souls for whom he is praying, as *Him to Whom* he
is praying. But the perfect love of God teaches him to find
souls in God Himself. He discovers that the soul which is
on fire with love for God actually loves herself and other
men more in proportion as she thinks about herself and
them less. Hence the paradox that the less the contemplative seems to love others and himself, the more he forgets
them in order to direct all his love to God, the more he
actually loves them and the better he serves their spiritual
interests. Loving God in God, the solitary is perfectly united
to that infinite Love with which God loves all things in
Himself. Loving all things in Him, the hermit powerfully
cooperates with the action of His love, drawing them to
Himself. Thus he fulfils most efficaciously the purpose of his
divine vocation which is to restore all things in Christ. Consequently the fruitfulness of the hermit in the Church of

God depends on his fidelity to the call to solitude, obscurity and abjection in Christ.

The doctrine of Paul Giustiniani is therefore a striking testimony to the primacy of contemplation and of the contemplative life in the Church.

It does not follow from this that everyone who aspires to perfection should therefore seek to become a hermit. The eremitical life is a charism reserved for few. Most monks will remain in the cenobium. Nevertheless, the fact that cenobitic life is safer and of wider appeal does not imply that the eremitical life is unsafe and has no appeal. The cenobium and the hermitage complete each other. If the cenobium disdains and repudiates the hermitage, it dooms itself to mediocrity. When the windows of the monastery no longer open out upon the vast horizons of the desert, the monastic community inevitably becomes immersed in vanity. All that is accidental, trivial, and accessory tends to assume a rank of high importance and to become the sole end of the monastic life. It is where monks have forgotten their potential destiny to solitude that they allow themselves to run to seed in bickering about curiosities, or squandering their contemplative leisure in material cares.

The doctrine of Paul Giustiniani should remind us all of the monk's true destiny as a man of God. True, Paul Giustiniani lacks the freshness of Cassian and the Desert Fathers, the luminous simplicity of St. Benedict, or St. Gregory, even more the sober enthusiasm of St. Bernard or the Greek Fathers. There is something in him of dryness which he contracted from the stoics and from scholastic philosophy. But the genuine spirit of the desert is there, and the contemplation which brightens his pages is unmistakably true.

In closing this preface, I might observe that it is perhaps

something altogether new and unusual for a book on an Italian hermit to appear, written by a Benedictine in Luxemburg and prefaced by a Cistercian in the southern United States. This joining together of Camaldoli, Monte-Corona, Clervaux and Gethsemani is surely significant. I dare to hope that it speaks very well for the union of the sons of St. Benedict with one another in our time—a union in prayer and deep charity and mutual understanding. If it be true, as I think it is, then our monasticism indeed has a function in the world. And it proclaims to all who will hear it the solemn affirmation of Christ who said: "Behold I am with you all days, even to the consummation of the world." [6]

[6] Matthew, 28:19.

NOTES FOR A
PHILOSOPHY OF SOLITUDE*

"Un cri d'oiseau sur les récifs ..."
ST. JOHN PERSE

ONE . *The tyranny of diversion*

1.   Why write about solitude in the first place? Certainly not in order to preach it, to exhort people to become

---

* This could also properly be called a "Philosophy of Monastic Life" if it be understood that a monk is, etymologically, a *monachos* or one who is isolated, alone. However since "monastic" now suggests not so much the man as the institution, I have seldom used the word "monk" in these pages. I am speaking of the solitary spirit which is really essential to the monastic view of life, but which is not confined to monasteries. Nor is it limited to men and women who have consecrated their lives to God by vow. Therefore, though I am treating of the traditional concept of the *monachos*, or solitary, I am deliberately discarding everything that can conjure up the artificial image of the monk in a cowl, dwelling in a medieval cloister. In this way I intend obviously, not to disparage or to reject the monastic institution, but to set aside all its accidentals and externals, so that they will not interfere with my view of what seems to me to be deepest and most essential. But by that same token, the "solitary" of these pages is never necessarily a "monk" (juridically) at all. He may well be a layman, and of the sort most remote from cloistered life, like Thoreau or Emily Dickenson.

solitary. What could be more absurd? Those who are to become solitary are, as a rule, solitary already. At most they are
not yet aware of their condition. In which case, all they need
is to discover it. But in reality, all men are solitary. Only most
of them are so averse to being alone, or to feeling alone, that
they do everything they can to forget their solitude. How?
Perhaps in large measure by what Pascal called "divertissement"—diversion, systematic distraction. By those occupations and recreations, so mercifully provided by society,
which enable a man to avoid his own company for twenty-
four hours a day.

Even the worst society has something about it that is not
only good, but essential for human life. Man cannot live without society, obviously. Those who claim they would like to do
so, or that they might be able to do so, are often those who
depend most abjectly upon it. Their pretense of solitude is
only an admission of their dependence. It is an individualis-
tic illusion.

Besides protecting man's natural life, enabling him to care
for himself, society gives each individual a chance to transcend himself in the service of others and thus to become a
person. But no one becomes a person merely by diversion—
in the sense of *divertissement*. For the function of diversion is simply to anesthetize the individual as individual, and
to plunge him in the warm, apathetic stupor of a collectivity
which, like himself, wishes to remain amused. The bread and
circuses which fulfil this function may be blatant and absurd,
or they may assume a hypocritical air of intense seriousness,
for instance in a mass movement. Our own society prefers the
absurd. But our absurdity is blended with a certain hard-
headed, fully determined seriousness with which we devote
ourselves to the acquisition of money, to the satisfaction of
our appetite for status, and our justification of ourselves as

contrasted with the totalitarian iniquity of our opposite number.

2. In a society like ours, there are obviously many people for whom solitude is a problem or even a temptation. I am perhaps in no position to resolve their problem or to exorcise their temptation. But it is possible that—knowing something at least of interior solitude—I might be able to say something of it which will reassure those tempted ones. At least I can suggest that if they have not been able to rest in the fervid consolations which are lavished upon them by society itself, that they do not need to seek such rest as that. They are perhaps perfectly capable of doing without such reassurance. They ought possibly to realize that they have less need of diversion than they are told, with such dogmatic self-complacency, by the organization men. They can confidently detach themselves from the engineers of the human soul whose talents are devoted to the cult of publicity Such an influence in their life is truly, as they tend to suspect, as unnecessary as it is irritating. But I do not promise to make it unavoidable.

Nor do I promise to cheer anybody up with optimistic answers to all the sordid difficulties and uncertainties which attend the life of interior solitude. Perhaps in the course of these reflections, some of the difficulties will be mentioned. The first of them has to be taken note of from the very start: the disconcerting task of facing and accepting one's own absurdity. The anguish of realizing that underneath the apparently logical pattern of a more or less "well organized" and rational life, there lies an abyss of irrationality, confusion, pointlessness, and indeed of apparent chaos. This is what immediately impresses itself upon the man who has renounced diversion. It cannot be otherwise: for in renouncing diversion, he renounces the seemingly harmless pleasure of building a tight, self-contained illusion about himself and about his little world. He accepts the difficulty of facing the million things in his life which are incomprehensible, instead of simply ignoring them. Incidentally it is only when the apparent absurdity of life is faced in all truth that faith really becomes possible. Otherwise, faith tends to be a kind of diversion, a spiritual amusement, in which one gathers up accepted, conventional formulas and arranges them in the approved mental patterns, without bothering to investigate their meaning, or asking if they have any practical consequences in one's life.

3.   One of the first essentials of the interior solitude of which I speak is that it is the actualization of a faith in which a man takes responsibility for his own inner life. He faces its full mystery, in the presence of the invisible God. And he takes upon himself the lonely, barely comprehensible, incommunicable task of working his way through the darkness of his own mystery until he discovers that his mystery and the mystery of God merge into one reality, which is the only reality. That God lives in him and he in God—not presicely in the way that words seem to suggest (for words have no power to comprehend the reality) but in a way that makes words, and even attempts to communicate, seem utterly illusory.

The words of God, the words which unite in "One Body" the society of those who truly believe, have the power to signify the mystery of our loneliness and oneness in Christ, to point the way into its darkness. They have the power, also, to illuminate the darkness. But they do so by losing the shape of words and becoming—not thoughts, not things, but the unspeakable beating of a Heart within the heart of one's own life.

4.   Every man is a solitary, held firmly by the inexorable

limitations of his own aloneness. Death makes this very clear, for when a man dies, he dies alone. The only one for whom the bell tolls, in all literal truth, is the one who is dying. It tolls "for thee" in so far as death is common to all of us, but obviously we do not all die at one and the same moment. We die *like* one another. The presence of many living men around the deathbed of one who is in agony may unite them all in the mystery of death, but it also unites them in a mystery of living solitude. It paradoxically unites them while reminding them acutely—and beyond words—of their isolation. Each one will have to die, and die *alone*. And, at the same time (but this is what they do not want to see) each one must also *live* alone. For we must remember that the Church is at the same time community and solitude. The dying Christian is one with the Church, but he also suffers the loneliness of Christ's agony in Gethsemani.

Very few men are able to face this fact squarely. And very few are expected to do so. It is the special vocation of certain ones who dedicate their whole lives to wrestling with solitude. An "agony" is a "wrestling." The dying man in agony wrestles with solitude. But the wrestling with one's solitude is also a life-work—a "life agony." When a man is called to be a solitary—(even if only interiorly)—he does not need to be anything else, nor can anything else be demanded of him except that he remain physically or spiritually alone fighting his battle which few can understand. His function in the Church—a social function and a spiritual one—is to remain in the "cell" of his aloneness, whether it be a real cell in the desert, or simply the spiritual cell of his own incomprehensible emptiness: and, as the desert fathers used to say, his "cell will teach him all things."

5.   The true solitary is not one who simply withdraws

from society. Mere withdrawal, regression, leads to a sick solitude, without meaning and without fruit. The solitary of whom I speak is called not to leave society but to transcend it: not to withdraw from the fellowship with other men but to renounce the appearance, the myth of union in diversion in order to attain to union on a higher and more spiritual level—the mystical level of the Body of Christ. He renounces that union with his immediate neighbors which is apparently achieved through the medium of the aspirations, fictions and conventions prevalent in his social group. But in so doing he attains to the basic, invisible, mysterious unity which makes all men "One Man" in Christ's Church beyond and in spite of natural social groups which, by their special myths and slogans, keep a man in a state of division.

The solitary, then has a mysterious and apparently absurd vocation to supernatural unity. He seeks a spiritual and simple oneness in himself which, when it is found, paradoxically becomes the oneness of all men—a oneness beyond separation, conflict and schism. For it is only when each man is one that mankind will once again become "One." But the solitary realizes that the images and myths of a particular group—projections of the interests, ideals and sins of that group—can take possession of him and divide him against himself.

The illusions and fictions encouraged by the appetite for self-affirmation in certain restricted groups, have much to be said for them and much to be said against them. They do in practice free a man from his individual limitations and help him, in some measure, to transcend himself. And if every society were ideal, then every society would help its members only to a fruitful and productive self-transcendence. But in fact societies tend to lift a man above himself only far enough to make him a useful and submissive instrument in whom the aspirations, lusts and needs of the group can function unhindered by too delicate a personal conscience. Social life tends to form and educate a man, but generally at the price of a simultaneous deformation and perversion. This is because civil society is never ideal, always a mixture of good and evil, and always tending to present the evil in itself as a form of good.

6.   There are crimes which no one would commit as an individual which he willingly and bravely commits when acting in the name of his society, because he has been (too easily) convinced that evil is entirely different when it is done "for the common good." As an example, one might point to the way in which racial hatreds and even persecution are admitted by people who consider themselves, and perhaps in some sense are, kind, tolerant, civilized and even humane. But they have acquired a special deformity of conscience as a result of their identification with their group, their immersion in their particular society. This deformation is the price they pay to forget and to exorcise that solitude which seems to them to be a demon.

7.   The solitary is one who is called to make one of the most terrible decisions possible to man: the decision to disagree completely with those who imagine that the call to diversion and self-deception is the voice of truth and who can summon the full authority of their own prejudice to prove it. He is therefore bound to sweat blood in anguish, in order to be loyal to God, to the Mystical Christ, and to humanity as a whole, rather than to the idol which is offered to him, for his homage, by a particular group. He must renounce the blessing of every convenient illusion that absolves him from responsibility when he is untrue to his deepest self and to his inmost truth—the image of God in his own soul.

The price of fidelity in such a task is a completely dedi-
cated humility—an emptiness of heart in which self-assertion
has no place. For if he is not empty and undivided in his
own inmost soul, the solitary will be nothing more than an
individualist. And in that case, his non-conformity is nothing but an act of rebellion: the substitution of idols and
illusions of his own choosing for those chosen by society.
And this, of course, is the greatest of dangers. It is both
futility and madness. It leads only to ruin.

For to forget oneself, at least to the extent of preferring
a social myth with a certain limited productiveness, is a
lesser evil than clinging to a private myth which is only
a sterile dream. And so, as Heraclitus said long ago, "We
must not act and speak like sleepers . . . The waking have
one common world, but the sleeping turn aside each into a
world of his own." Hence the vocation to solitude is not a
vocation to the warm narcissistic dream of a private religion. It is a vocation to become *fully awake*, even more than
the common somnolence permits one to be, with its arbitrary selection of approved dreams, mixed with a few really
valid and fruitful conceptions.

8.   It should be clear from the start then that the solitary worthy of the name lives not in a world of private
fictions and self-constructed delusions, but in a world of
emptiness, humility, and purity beyond the reach of slogans
and beyond the gravitational pull of diversions that alienate
him from God and from himself. He lives in unity. His
solitude is neither an argument, an accusation, a reproach
or a sermon. It is simply itself. It *is*. And therefore it not
only does not attract attention, or desire it, but it remains, for
the most part, completely invisible.

9.   It should be quite clear then, that there is no
question in these pages of the eccentric and regressive

solitude that clamors for recognition, and which seeks to focus more pleasurably and more intently on itself by stepping back from the crowd. But unfortunately, however often I may repeat this warning, it will not be heeded. Those who most need to hear it are incapable of doing so. They think that solitude is a heightening of self-consciousness an intensification of pleasure in self. It is a more secret and more perfect diversion. What they want is not the hidden, metaphysical agony of the hermit but the noisy self-congratulations and self-pity of the infant in the cradle. Ultimately what they want is not the desert but the womb.

The individualist in practice completely accepts the social fictions around him, but accepts them in such a way that they provide a suitable background against which a few private and favored fictions of his own can make an appearance. Without the social background, his individual fictions would not be able to assert themselves, and he himself would no longer be able to fix his attention upon them.

TWO . *In the sea of perils*

1.   There is no need to say that the call of solitude (even though only interior) is perilous. Everyone who knows what solitude means is aware of this. The essence of the solitary vocation is precisely the anguish of an almost infinite risk. Only the false solitary sees no danger in solitude. But his solitude is imaginary, that is to say built around an image. It is merely a social image stripped of its explicitly social elements. The false solitary is one who is able to imagine himself without companions while in reality he remains just as dependent on society as before—if not more dependent. He needs society as a ventriloquist needs a

dummy. He projects his own voice to the group and it comes
back to him admiring, approving, opposing or at least ad-
verting to his own separateness.

Even if society seems to condemn him, this pleases and
diverts him for it is nothing but the sound of his own
voice, reminding him of his separateness, which is his chosen
diversion. True solitude is not mere separateness. It tends
only to *unity*.

2.   The true solitary does not renounce anything that
is basic and human about his relationship to other men. He
is deeply united to them—all the more deeply because he is
no longer entranced by marginal concerns. What he renounces is the superficial imagery and the trite symbolism
that pretend to make the relationship more genuine and
more fruitful. He gives up his lax self-abandonment to general diversion. He renounces vain pretenses of solidarity that
tend to substitute themselves for real solidarity, while mask-
ing an inner spirit of irresponsibility and selfishness. He renounces illusory claims of collective achievement and fulfilment, by which society seeks to gratify and assuage the individual's need to feel that he amounts to something.

The man who is dominated by what I have called the
"social image" is one who allows himself to see and to approve in himself only that which his society prescribes as
beneficial and praiseworthy in its members. As a corollary
he sees and disapproves (usually in *others*) mostly what his
society disapproves. And yet he congratulates himself on
"thinking for himself." In reality, this is only a game that
he plays in his own mind—the game of substituting the
words, slogans and concepts he has received from society,
for genuine experiences of his own. Or rather—the slogans of
society are felt to rise up within him as if they were his own,
"spontaneous experience." How can such a man be really "so-

cial"? He is imprisoned in an illusion and cut off from real, living contact with his fellow man. Yet he does not feel himself to be in any way "alone!"

3.   The solitary is first of all one who renounces this arbitrary social imagery. When his nation wins a war or sends a rocket to the moon, he can get along without feeling as if he personally had won the war or hit the moon with a rocket. When his nation is rich and arrogant, he does not feel that he himself is more fortunate and more honest, as well as more powerful than the citizens of other, more "backward" nations. More than this: he is able to despise war and to see the futility of rockets to the moon in a way quite different and more fundamental from the way in which his society may tolerate these negative views. That is to say, he despises the criminal, bloodthirsty arrogance of his own nation or class, as much as that of "the enemy." He despises his own self-seeking aggressivity as much as that of the politicians who hypocritically pretend they are fighting for peace.

4.   Most men cannot live fruitfully without a large proportion of fiction in their thinking. If they do not have some efficacious mythology around which to organize their activities, they will regress into a less efficacious, more primitive, more chaotic set of illusions. When the ancients said that the solitary was likely to be either a god or a beast, they meant that he would either achieve a rare intellectual and spiritual independence, or sink into a more complete and brutish dependence. The solitary easily plunges into a cavern of darkness and of phantoms more horrible and more absurd than the most inane set of conventional social images. The suffering he must then face is neither salutary nor noble. It is catastrophic.

5.   I do not pretend, in these pages to establish a

clear formula for discerning solitary vocations. But this
much needs to be said: that one who is called to solitude is
not called merely to imagine himself solitary, to live as if he
were solitary, to cultivate the illusion that he is different,
withdrawn and elevated. He is called to emptiness. And in
this emptiness he does not find points upon which to base a
contrast between himself and others. On the contrary, he
realizes, though perhaps confusedly, that he has entered into
a *solitude that is really shared by everyone*. It is not that he
is solitary while everybody else is social: but that everyone
is solitary, in a solitude masked by that symbolism which
they use to cheat and counteract their solitariness. What the
solitary renounces is not his union with other men, but
rather the deceptive fictions and inadequate symbols which
tend to take the place of genuine social unity—to produce a
façade of apparent unity without really uniting men on a
deep level. Example—the excitement and fictitious engage-
ment of a football crowd. This is to say, of course, that the
Christian solitary is fully and perfectly a man of the Church.

Even though he may be physically alone the solitary remains united to others and lives in profound solidarity with
them, but on a deeper and mystical level. They may think
he is one with them in the vain interests and preoccupations
of a superficial social existence. He realizes that he is one
with them in the peril and anguish of their common solitude: not the solitude of the individual only, but the radical
and essential *solitude of man*—a solitude which was as-
sumed by Christ and which, in Christ, becomes mysteriously identified with the solitude of God.

6.   The solitary is one who is aware of solitude in himself as a basic and inevitable human reality, not just as
something which affects him as an isolated individual.
Hence his solitude is the foundation of a deep, pure and

gentle sympathy with all other men, whether or not they are capable of realizing the tragedy of their plight. More—it is the doorway by which he enters into the mystery of God, and brings others into that mystery by the power of his love and his humility.

7.   The emptiness of the true solitary is marked then by a great simplicity. This simplicity can be deceptive, because it may be hidden under a surface of apparent complexity, but it is there nevertheless, behind the outer contradictions of the man's life. It manifests itself in a kind of candor though he may be very reticent. There is in this lonely one a gentleness, a deep sympathy, though he may be apparently unsocial. There is a great purity of love, though he may hesitate to manifest his love in any way, or to commit himself openly to it. Underneath the complications that are produced in him by his uneasiness with social images, the man tends to live without images, without too much conceptual thought. When you get to know him well—which is sometimes possible—you may find in him not so much a man who seeks solitude as one who has already found it, or been found by it. His problem then is not to find what he already has, but to discover what to do about it.

8.   One who has made the discovery of his inner solitude, or is just about to make it, may need considerable spiritual help. A wise man, who knows the plight of the new solitary, may with the right word at the right time spare him the pain of seeking vainly some long and complex statement of his case. No such statement is necessary: he has simply discovered what it means to be a man. And he has begun to realize that what he sees in himself is not a spiritual luxury but a difficult, humiliating responsibility: the obligation to be spiritually mature.

9.   The solitary condition also has its jargon and its

conventions: these too are pitiful. There is no point in consoling one who has awakened to his solitude by teaching him to defile his emptiness with rationalizations. Solitude must not become a diversion to itself by too much self-justification. At least allow the° lonely one to meet his emptiness and come to terms with it: for it is really his destiny and his joy. Too many people are ready to draw him back at any price from what they conceive to be the edge of the abyss. True, it is an abyss: but they do not realize that he who is called to solitude is called to walk across the air of the abyss without danger, because, after all, the abyss is only himself. He should not be forced to feel guilty about it, for in this solitude and emptiness of his heart there is another, more inexplicable solitude. Man's loneliness is, in fact, the loneliness of God. That is why it is such a great thing for a man to discover his solitude and learn to live in it. For there he finds that he and God are one: that God is alone as he himself is alone. That God wills to be alone in him.

When this is understood, then one sees that his duty is to be faithful to solitude because in this way he is faithful to God. Fidelity is everything. From it the solitary can expect truth and strength, light and wisdom at the right time. If he is not faithful to the inner anonymity and emptiness which are the secret of his whole life, then he can expect nothing but confusion.

10.   Like everything else in the Christian life, the vocation to spiritual solitude can be understood only within the perspectives of God's mercy to man in the Incarnation of Christ. If there is any such thing as a Christian hermit, then he must be a man who has a special function in the mystical body of Christ—a hidden and spiritual function, and perhaps all the more vital because more hidden. But this

social function of the solitary contemplative, precisely because it has to be invisible, cannot be allowed in any way to detract from his genuinely solitary character. On the contrary, his function in the Christian community is the paradoxical one of living outwardly separated from the community. And this, whether he is conscious of it or not, is a witness to the completely transcendental character of the Christian mystery of our unity in Christ.

The hermit remains to put us on our guard against our natural obsession with the visible, social and communal forms of Christian life which tend at times to be inordinately active, and often become deeply involved in the life of secular, non-Christian society. It is true to say of every Christian that he is in the world but not of it. But in case he might be likely to forget this—or worse still in case he might never come to know it at all—there must be men who have completely renounced the world: men who are neither in the world nor of it. In our day, when "the world" is everywhere, even in the desert where it makes and proves its secret weapons, the solitary retains his unique and mysterious function. But he will fulfil it perhaps in many paradoxical ways. Wherever he does so, even where he is unseen, he testifies to the essentially mystical bond of unity which binds Christians together in the Holy Spirit. Whether he is seen or not, he bears witness to the unity of Christ by possessing in himself the fullness of Christian charity.

In fact, the early Christians who went into the desert to see the hermits of Nitria and Scete admired in them not so much their extreme asceticism as their charity and discretion. The miracle of the Desert Fathers was precisely that a man could live entirely separate from the visible Christian community with its normal liturgical functions, and still be full of the charity of Christ. He was able to be so only

because he was completely empty of himself. The vocation to
solitude is therefore at the same time a vocation to silence,
poverty and emptiness. But the emptiness is for the sake of
fulness: the purpose of the solitary life is, if you like, contemplation. But not contemplation in the pagan sense of an
intellectual, esoteric enlightenment, achieved by ascetic
technique. The contemplation of the Christian solitary is the
awareness of the divine mercy transforming and elevating his
own emptiness and turning it into the presence of perfect
love, perfect fulness.

Hence a Christian can turn his back on society, even on
the society of his fellow Christians, without necessarily hating
society. This is because of the spiritual and mystical character of the Christian Church—the same spiritual character
which accounts for the fact that one who renounces marriage in order to be a priest or a monk can thereby, if he is
faithful, attain to a higher and more spiritual fruitfulness.
So a Christian hermit can, by being alone, paradoxically
live even closer to the heart of the Church than one who is in
the midst of her apostolic activities. The life and unity of the
Church are, and must be, visible. But that does not mean
that the invisible and spiritual activities of men of prayer are
not supremely important. On the contrary, the invisible
and more mysterious life of prayer is *essential* to the Church.
Solitaries, too, are essential to her!

11.   Withdrawal from other men can be a special form
of love for them. It should never be a rejection of man or of
his society. But it may well be a quiet and humble refusal
to accept the myths and fictions with which social life cannot help but be full—especially today. To despair of the
illusions and façades which man builds around himself is
certainly not to despair of man. On the contrary, it may be
a sign of love and of hope. For when we love someone,

we refuse to tolerate what destroys and maims his personality. If we love mankind, can we blind ourselves to man's predicament? You will say: we must do something about his predicament. But there are some whose vocation it is to realize that they, at least, cannot help in any overt social way. Their contribution is a mute witness, a secret and even invisible expression of love which takes the form of their own option for solitude in preference to the acceptance of social fictions. For is not our involvement in fiction, particularly in political and demagogic fiction, and implicit confession that we despair of man and even of God?

12.   Christian hope in God and in the world to come is inevitably also hope in man, or at least *for* man. How can we despair of man when the Word of God was made man in order to save us all? But our Christian hope is, and must remain, inviolably pure. It must work and struggle in the chaos of conflicting policy which is the world of egotism: and in order to do so it must take on visible, symbolic forms by which to declare its message. But when these symbols become confused with other secular symbols, then there is danger that faith itself will be corrupted by fictions, and there is a consequent obligation, on the part of some Christians, to affirm their faith in all its intransigent purity.

At such a time, some men will seek clarity in isolation and silence, not because they think they know better than the rest, but because they want to see life in a different perspective. They want to withdraw from the babel of confusion in order to listen more patiently to the voice of their conscience and to the Holy Spirit. And by their prayers and their fidelity they will invisibly renew the life of the whole Church. This renewal will communicate itself to others who remain "in the world" and will help them also to regain a clearer vision, a sharper and more unpromising appreciation of Christian truth. These will give themselves to apostolic work on a new level of seriousness and of faith. They will be able to discard fictitious gestures of zeal in favor of genuine self-sacrificing love. So when, as in our time, the whole world seems to have become one immense and idiotic fiction, and when the virus of mendacity creeps into every vein and organ of the social body, it would be abnormal and immoral if there were no reaction. It is even healthy that the reaction should sometimes take the form of outspoken protest, as long as we remember that solitude is no refuge for the rebellious. And if there is an element of protest in the solitary vocation, that element must be a matter of rigorous spirituality. It must be deep and interior, and intimately personal, so that the solitary is one who is critical, first of all, of himself. Otherwise he will divert himself with a fiction worse than that of all the others, becoming a more insane and self-opinionated liar than the worst of them, cheating no one more than himself. Solitude is not for rebels like this, and it promptly rejects them. The desert is for those who have felt a salutary despair of conventional and fictitious values, in order to hope in mercy and to be themselves merciful men to whom that mercy is promised. Such solitaries know the evils that are in other men because they experience these evils first of all in themselves.

Such men, out of pity for the universe, out of loyalty to mankind, and without a spirit of bitterness or of resentment, withdraw into the healing silence of the wilderness, or of poverty, or of obscurity, not in order to preach to others but to heal in themselves the wounds of the entire world.

13.   The message of God's mercy to man must be preached. The word of truth must be proclaimed. No one can deny this. But there are not a few who are beginning to feel the futility of adding more words to the constant flood of language that pours meaninglessly over everybody, everywhere,

from morning to night. For language to have meaning, there must be intervals of silence somewhere, to divide word from word and utterance from utterance. He who retires into silence does not necessarily hate language. Perhaps it is love and respect for language which impose silence upon him. For the mercy of God is not heard in words unless it is heard, both before and after the words are spoken, in silence.

14.   There have always been, and always will be, men who are alone in the midst of society without realizing why. They are condemned to their strange isolation by temperament or circumstance, and they get used to it. It is not of these that I am speaking, but of those who having led active and articulate lives in the world of men, leave their old life behind and go into the desert. The desert does not necessarily have to be physical—it can be found even in the midst of men. But it is not found by human aspirations or idealism. It is mysteriously designated by the finger of God.

15.   There have always been solitaries who, by virtue of a special purity, and simplicity of heart, have been destined from their earliest youth to an eremitical and contemplative life, in some official form. These are the clear, uncomplicated vocations, and I do not speak explicitly of them here either. They have known from an early age that their destination was a Charterhouse or a Camaldolese cell. Or they have found their way, as though by unerring instinct, into the place where they will be alone. The Church has welcomed these without question and without trouble into the "shadowy" (*umbratilis*) life of peace which she has reserved for her most favored children. There, in the peace and silence of a solitude fully recognized, protected and approved by the Highest Authority of the Church, they live their lives, not without the sufferings and the complexities

which in solitude are unavoidable, but in a peace and assurance which are a rare guarantee of a truly special vocation.

It is not of these that I speak but of the paradoxical, tormented solitaries for whom there is no real place; men and women who have not so much chosen solitude as been chosen by it. And these have not generally found their way into the desert either through simplicity or through innocence. Theirs is the solitude that is reached the hard way, through bitter suffering and disillusionment.

To say that they have been "found" and chosen by solitude is a metaphor that must not be taken to mean that they have been drawn into it entirely passively. The solitude of which I speak is not full grown and true until it has been elected by a deep interior decision. Solitude may choose and select a man for herself, but he is not hers unless he has accepted. On the other hand no amount of deciding will do any good, if one has not first been invited to make the decision. The door to solitude opens only from the inside. This is true of both solitudes, the exterior and the interior. No matter how alone one may be, if he has not been invited ot interior solitude and accepted the invitation with full consciousness of what he is doing, he cannot be what I call a *monachos*, or solitary. But one who has made this choice and kept to it is always alone, no matter how many people there may be around him. Not that he is withdrawn from them, or that he is not one of them. His solitude is not of that order at all. It does not set him apart from them in contrast and self-affirmation. It affirms nothing. It is at the same time empty and universal. He is one, not by virtue of separation but by virtue of inner spiritual unity. And this inner unity is at the same time the inner unity of all. Needless to say, such unity is secret and unknown. Even those who enter it, know it only, so to speak, by "unknowing."

It should therefore be clear that one who seeks to enter into this kind of solitude by affirming himself, and separating himself from others, and intensifying his awareness of his own individual being, is only travelling further and further away from it. But the one who has been found by solitude, and invited to enter it, and has entered freely, falls into the desert the way a ripe fruit falls out of a tree. It does not matter what kind of a desert it may be: in the midst of men or far from them. It is the one vast desert of emptiness which belongs to no one and to everyone. It is the place of silence where one word is spoken by God. And in that word are spoken both God Himself and all things.

16.   Often the lonely and the empty have found their way into this pure silence only after many false starts. They have taken many wrong roads, even roads that were totally alien to their character and vocation. They have repeatedly contradicted themselves and their own inmost truth. Their very nature seems itself to be a contradiction. They have perhaps few "clear signs" of *any* vocation. But they end up nevertheless alone. Their way is to have no way. Their destiny is poverty, emptiness, anonymity.

17.   Of course, everyone with any sense sees, from time to time, in a lucid moment, the folly and triviality of our conventionalized attitudes. It is possible for anyone to dream of liberty. But to undertake the wretched austerity of living in complete honesty, without convention and therefore without support, is quite another matter. That is why there exist communities of beatniks, of esoteric thinkers and cultists, of quasi-religious faddists, of western followers of oriental religions. The break with the big group is compensated

by enrollment in the little group. It is a flight not into solitude but into a protesting minority. Such a flight may be more or less honest, more or less honorable. Certainly it inspires the anger of those who believe themselves to be the "right thinking majority" and it necessarily comes in for its fair share of mockery on that account. Perhaps this mockery is so welcome as to contribute, negatively, to the process of falsification and corruption which these groups almost always undergo. They abandon one illusion which is forced on everyone and substitute for it another, more esoteric illusion, of their own making. They have the satisfaction of making a choice, but not the fulfilment of having chosen reality.

18.   The true solitary is not called to an illusion, to the contemplation of himself as solitary. He is called to the nakedness and hunger of a more primitive and honest condition. The condition of a stranger (*xeniteia*) and a wanderer on the face of the earth, who has been called out of what was familiar to him in order to seek strangely and painfully after he knows not what.

And in demanding "honesty" of the hermit, let us not be too hypocritically exacting. He too may have his eccentricities. He may rely heavily on certain imperfect solutions to problems which his human weakness does not allow him to cope with fully. Let us not condemn him for failing to solve problems we have not even dared to face.

The solitary life is an arid, rugged purification of the heart. St. Jerome and St. Eucherius have written rhapsodies about the flowering desert, but Jerome was the busiest hermit that ever lived and Eucherius was a bishop who admired the hermit brethren of Lerins only from afar. The *eremi cultores*, the farmers of the desert sand, have had less to say about the experience. They have been washed out by dryness, and their burnt lips are weary of speech.

19. The solitary who no longer communicates with other men except for the bare necessities of life is a man with a special and difficult task. He is called to be, in some way, invisible. He soon loses all sense of his significance for the rest of the world. And yet that significance is great. The hermit has a very real place in a world like ours that has degraded the human person and lost all respect for that awesome loneliness in which each single spirit must confront the living God.

20. In the eyes of our conformist society, the hermit is nothing but a failure. He has to be a failure—we have absolutely no use for him, no place for him. He is outside all our projects, plans, assemblies, movements. We can countenance him as long as he remains only a fiction, or a dream. As soon as he becomes real, we are revolted by his insignificance, his poverty, his shabbiness, his total lack of status. Even those who consider themselves contemplatives, often cherish a secret contempt for the solitary. For in the contemplative life of the hermit there is none of that noble security, that intelligent depth, that artistic finesse which the more academic contemplative seeks in his sedate respectability.

21. It has never been either practical or useful to leave all things and follow Christ. And yet it is spiritually prudent. Practical utility and supernatural prudence are sometimes flatly opposed to one another, as wisdom of the flesh and prudence of the spirit. Not that the spirit can never allow itself to accomplish things in a practical, temporal way. But it does not rest in purely temporal ends. Its accomplishments belong to a higher and more spiritual order—which is of course necessarily hidden. Practical utility has its roots in the present life. Supernatural prudence lives for the world to come. It weighs all things in the balance of eternity. Spiritual things have no weight for the "practical" man. The

solitary life is something that cannot even tip his scales. It is "nothing," a non-entity. Yet St Paul says: "The foolish things of the world hath God chosen that He may confound the wise, and the weak things of the world hath God chosen that He may confound the strong. And the base things of the world, and the things that are contemptible hath God chosen, and things that are not, that He might bring to nought things that are." (I Corinthians, 1:27,28)

And why is this? "That no flesh should glory in His sight." It is the invisible glory that is real. The empty horizons of the solitary life enable us to grow accustomed to a light that is not seen where the mirage of secular pursuits fascinates and deludes our gaze.

22.   The hermit remains there to prove, by his lack of practical utility and the apparent sterility of his vocation, that cenobitic monks themselves ought to have little significance in the world, or indeed none at all. They are dead to the world, they should no longer cut a figure in it. And the world is dead to them. They are pilgrims in it, isolated witnesses of another kingdom. This of course is the price they pay for universal compassion, for a sympathy that reaches all. The monk is compassionate in proportion as he is less practical and less successful, because the job of being a success in a competitive society leaves one no time for compassion.

The monk has all the more of a part to play in our world, because he has no proper place in it.

THREE . *Spiritual poverty*

1.   One of the most telling criticisms of the solitary may well be that even in his life of prayer he is less "productive." You would think that in his solitude he would

quickly reach the level of visions, of mystical marriage, something dramatic at any rate. Yet he may well be poorer than the cenobite, *even in his life of prayer*. His is a weak and precarious existence, he has more cares, he is more insecure, he has to struggle to preserve himself from all kinds of petty annoyances, and often he fails to do so. His poverty is spiritual. It invades his whole soul as well as his body, and in the end his whole patrimony is one of insecurity. He enjoys the sorrow, the spiritual and intellectual indigence of the really poor. Obviously such a vocation has in it a grain of folly. Otherwise it is not what it is meant to be, a life of direct dependence on God, in darkness, insecurity and pure faith. The life of the hermit is a life of material and physical poverty without visible support.

2.   Of course, one must not exaggerate or be too absolute in this matter. Absolutism itself can become a kind of "fortune" and "honor." We must also face the fact that the average human being is incapable of a life in which austerity is without compromise. There comes a limit, beyond which human weakness cannot go, and where mitigation itself enters in as a subtle form of poverty. Maybe the hermit turns out, unaccountably, to have his ulcer just like the next man. No doubt he has to drink large quantities of milk and perhaps take medicines. This finally disposes of any hope of him becoming a legendary figure. He, too, worries. Perhaps he worries even more than others, for it is only in the minds of those who know nothing about it that the solitary life appears to be a life free from all care.

3.   We must remember that Robinson Crusoe was one of the great myths of the middle class, commercial civilization of the eighteenth and nineteenth centuries: the myth not of eremitical solitude but of pragmatic individualism. Crusoe is a symbolical figure in an era when every man's

house was his castle in the trees, but only because every man was a very prudent and resourceful citizen who knew how to make the best out of the least and could drive a hard bargain with any competitor, even life itself. Carefree Crusoe was happy because he had an answer to everything. The real hermit is not so sure he has an answer.

4.   It is true that the solitary life must also be a life of prayer and meditation, if it is to be authentically Christian. For the *monachos* in our context is purely and simply a man of God. This should be clear. But what prayer! What meditation! Nothing more like bread and water than this interior prayer of his! Utter poverty. Often an incapacity to pray, to see, to hope. Not the sweet passivity which the books extol, but a bitter, arid struggle to press forward through a blinding sandstorm. The solitary may well beat his head against a wall of doubt. That may be the full extent of his contemplation. Do not mistake my meaning. It is not a question of intellectual doubt, an analytical investigation of the theological, philosophical or some other truths. It is something else, a kind of unknowing of his own self, a kind of doubt that questions the very roots of his own existence, a doubt which undermines his very reasons for existing and for doing what he does. It is this doubt which reduces him finally to silence, and in the silence which ceases to ask questions, he receives the only certitude he knows: The presence of God in the midst of uncertainty and nothingness, as the only reality but as a reality which cannot be "placed" or identified.

Hence the solitary man says nothing, and does his work, and is patient, (or perhaps impatient, I don't know) but generally he has peace. It is not the world's kind of peace. He is happy, but he never has a good time. He knows where he is going, but he is not "sure of his way," he just knows by going there. He does not see the way beforehand, and when he arrives, he arrives. His arrivals are usually departures from anything that resembles a "way." That is his way. But he cannot understand it. Neither can we.

5. Beyond and in all this, he possesses his solitude, the riches of his emptiness, his interior poverty but of course, it is not a possession. It is simply an established fact. It is there. It is assured. In fact, it is inescapable. It is everything. It contains God, surrounds him in God, plunges him in God. So great is his poverty that he does not even see God: so great are his riches that he is lost in God and lost to himself. He is never far enough away from God to see Him in perspective, or as an object. He is swallowed up in Him, and therefore so to speak, never sees Him at all.

6. All that we can say of this indigence of the lonely life must not make us forget the fact that this man is happy in his solitude, but especially because he has ceased to regard himself as a solitary in contradistinction to others who are not solitary. He simply is. And if he has been impoverished and set aside by the will of God, this is not a distinction, but purely and simply a fact. His solitude is sometimes frightening, sometimes a burden, yet it is more precious to him than anything else because it is for him the will of God,—not a thing willed by God, not an object decreed by a remote power, but simply the pressure, upon his own life, of that pure actuality which is the will of God, the reality of all that is real. His solitude is, for him simply reality. He could not break away from this will even if he wanted to. To be prisoner of this love is to be free, and almost to be in paradise. Hence the life of solitude is a life of love without consolation, a life that is fruitful because it is pressed down

and running over with the will of God: and all that has his will in it is full of significance, even when it appears to make no sense at all.

7.   The terror of the lonely life is the mystery and uncertainty with which the will of God presses upon our soul. It is much easier, and gentler, and more secure to have the will of God filtered to us quietly through society, through decrees of men, through the orders of others. To take this will straight in all its incomprehensible, baffling mystery, is not possible to one who is not secretly protected and guided by the Holy Spirit and no one should try it unless he has some assurance that he really has been called to it by God. And this call, of course, should be made clear by Directors and Superiors. One has to be born into solitude carefully, patiently and after long delay, out of the womb of society. One cannot rashly presume to become a solitary merely by his own will. This is no security outside the guidance of the Church.

8.   The lone man remains in the world as a prophet to whom no one listens as a voice crying in the desert, as a sign of contradiction. The world necessarily rejects him and in that act, rejects the dreaded solitude of God Himself. For that is what the world resents about God: His utter otherness, His absolute incapacity to be absorbed into the context of worldly and practical slogans, His mysterious transcendency which places Him infinitely beyond the reach of catchwords, advertisements and politics. It is easier for the world to recreate a god in its own image, a god who justifies its own slogans, when there are no solitaries about to remind men of the solitude of God: the God Who cannot become a member of any purely human fellowship. And yet this Solitary God has called men to another fellowship, with Himself, through the Passion and Resurrection of Christ—

through the solitude of Gethsemani and of Cavalry, and the mystery of Easter, and the solitude of the Ascension: all of which precede the great communion of Pentecost.

9.   The lonely man's function is to remain in existence as solitary, as poor and as unacceptable as God Himself in the souls of so many men. The solitary is there to tell them, in a way they can barely understand, that if they were able to discover and appreciate their own inner solitude they would immediately discover God and find out, from His word to them, that they are really persons.

10.   It is often said that exterior solitude is not only dangerous, but totally unnecessary. Unnecessary because all that really matters is interior solitude. And this can be obtained without physical isolation.

There is in this statement a truth more terrible than can be imagined by those who make it, so readily and with so little awareness of the irony implicit in their words.

11.   Indeed there is a special irony about solitude in community: that if you are called to solitude by God, even if you live in a community your solitude will be inescapable. Even if you are surrounded by the comfort and the assistance of others, the bonds that unite you with them on a trivial level break one by one so that you are no longer supported by them, that is, no longer sustained by the instinctive, automatic mechanisms of collective life. Their words, their enthusiasms become meaningless. Yet you do not despise them, or reject them. You try to find if there is not still some way to comprehend them and live by them. And you find that words have no value in such a situation. The only thing that can help you is the deep, wordless communion of genuine love.

At such a time it is a great relief to be put in contact with others by some simple task, some function of the ministry.

Then you meet them not with your words or theirs, but with the words and sacramental gestures of God. The word of God takes on an ineffable purity and strength when it is seen as the only way in which a solitary can effectively reach the solitudes of others—the solitudes of which these others are unaware.

Then he realizes that he loves them more than ever: perhaps that he now loves them really for the first time. Made humble by his solitude, grateful for the work that brings him into contact with others, he still remains alone. There is no greater loneliness than that of an instrument of God who realizes that his words and his ministry, even though they be the words of God, can do nothing to change his loneliness: and yet that, beyond all distinction between mine and thine, they make him one with everyone he encounters.

12.   What then is the conclusion? That this solitude of which we have been speaking, the solitude of the true *monachos*, of the lone one, is not and cannot be selfish. It is the opposite of selfish. It is the death and the forgetfulness of self. But what is self? The self that vanishes from this emptiness is the superficial, false social self, the image made up of the prejudices, the whimsey, the posturing, the pharisaic self-concern and the pseudo dedication which are the heritage of the individual in a limited and imperfect group.

There is another self, a true self, who comes to full maturity in emptiness and solitude—and who can of course, begin to appear and grow in the valid, sacrificial and creative self-dedication that belong to a genuine social existence. But note that even this social maturing of love implies at the same time the growth of a certain inner solitude.

Without solitude of some sort there is and can be no maturity. Unless one becomes empty and alone, he cannot give himself in love because he does not possess the deep self which is the only gift worthy of love. And this deep self, we immediately add, cannot be *possessed*. My deep self is not "something" which I acquire, or to which I "attain" after a long struggle. It is not mine, and cannot become mine. It is no "thing"—no object. It is "I."

The shallow "I" of individualism can be possessed, developed, cultivated, pandered to, satisfied: it is the center of all our strivings for gain and for satisfaction, whether material or spiritual. But the deep "I" of the spirit, of solitude and of love, cannot be "had," possessed, developed, perfected. It can only *be*, and *act* according to deep inner laws which are not of man's contriving, but which come from God. They are the Laws of the Spirit, who, like the wind, glows where He wills. This inner "I," who is always alone, is always universal: for in this inmost "I" my own solitude meets the solitude of every other man and the solitude of God. Hence it is beyond division, beyond limitation, beyond selfish affirmation. It is only this inmost and solitary "I" that truly loves with the love and the spirit of Christ. This "I" is Christ Himself, living in us: and we, in Him, living in the Father.

LIGHT IN DARKNESS

The Ascetic Doctrine of St. John of the Cross

In understanding the sanctity and Doctrine of St. John of the Cross, the first thing we must do is to see them in the clear perspectives of the New Testament, the Sermon on the Mount, the profound discourses in the Gospel of St. John, and particularly the mystery of the Passion and the Resurrection of the Son of God. In this way, we will be preserved from the danger of giving the writings of the Carmelite Doctor a kind of stoical bias which makes his austerity seem pointlessly inhuman, and which, instead of opening our hearts to divine grace closes them in upon themselves in fanatical rigidity.

There are plenty of "hard sayings" in St. John of the Cross, just as there were hard sayings in the Gospel. Our Lord said that we must "hate our Father and Mother . . . and even our own life." But we know that the hard sayings in the Gospel need to be properly qualified and understood. The command to "hate" father and mother, which at times

seems so scandalous, does not interfere with the commandment to love and revere them. It is simply a strong statement of the hierarchy of value for the Christian—in which
the salvation of his own soul comes before everything else,
and in which, *if there arises a choice* between the love of
parents and the love of truth, or the love of one's own life
and fidelity to the word of God, then one's natural love
must be sacrificed.

This same principle will serve to explain many of the
seemingly harsh and extreme statements of St. John of the
Cross. His whole asceticism is basically a question of choice,
of preference. And we cannot understand what he is talking
about if we do not see what the choice really is. On the one
hand, the love and the will of God: on the other, the love
and the gratification of self. But what do these alternatives
mean *in practice?* If we merely take them in the abstract,
then the asceticism of St. John of the Cross becomes something mechanical, cold, soulless and inhuman: a kind of
mathematical exclusion of all spontaneity in favor of dreary
and rigid self-punishment. But if we see what he is talking
about in the concrete, it is quite a different matter. For on
the one hand, we have the confused, dissipated, and unruly
urges of our indisciplined desire, which draw us into a state
of blindness, weariness, distraction and exile from God. On
the other hand there are the very real and very urgent in-
spirations of the Holy Spirit of Divine Wisdom, that "loving, tranquil, lonely and peaceful sweet inebriator of the
spirit. Hereby the soul feels itself to be gently and tenderly
wounded and ravished, knowing not by whom, nor whence,
nor how." (*Living Flame of Love,* iii, 38 Vol III p. 181)
One who does not genuinely experience in himself the
reality of these two alternatives cannot fully appreciate the
ascetic teaching of St. John of the Cross. However, even

those who are not themselves mystics can profit by reading his works, if only they remember to see them in perspective.

When St. John of the Cross says, for instance, that we must treat our companions in the monastery as if they were not there, he can be tragically misunderstood by anyone who does not know precisely what the saint is aiming at. He certainly does not mean that we could simply stifle our spontaneous love and live like creatures without sensibility or affection. This would, in fact, be a sin not only against charity but even against temperance. (Insensibility is a sin against temperance, says St. Thomas: II II Q. 142 a.1) On the contrary, St. John *presumes* a very special situation: a community of contemplatives in which all have a definite call to "enjoy" the much higher and more spiritual form of love that we have suggested above. This secret, silent, contemplative union with God does not in fact exclude fraternal union but on the contrary it contains it within itself. Those who live the contemplative life on this level, are all the more closely united with one another in proportion as they grow in spiritual union with God. Therefore St. John of the Cross is certainly very wise in warning them against the temptation to become too preoccupied with one another on a more exterior, more conventional level, which would in fact keep them from growing in true delicacy of love. Experience in the contemplative life shows us that spiritual confusion awaits those who yield to foolish and sentimental impulse under the guise of charity, and allow themselves to lose their first fruits of prayer in an absurdly useless preoccupation with the lives of those around them. They become nothing else but sentimental busybodies, interfering with the order of the community, the peace of their companions, and the secret action of the Holy Spirit. Sometimes this false charity procedes from a hidden sensuality, and in other cases it is an expression of latent activism, an attempt to escape from the interior solitude of the contemplative with the deprivations it implies. Such temptations are quite natural, of course: but a spirituality that is basically active and extraverted will not help one to meet the problem in a contemplative way. St. John of the Cross firmly and resolutely sticks to his viewpoint. His way may seem drastic, but it can lead one to the interior detachment and tranquility without which a fully contemplative life is impossible.

Seen in this light, the *Cautions*, addressed to the community of nuns which the saint directed at Beas in Andalusia, is likely to be interpreted more wisely. The same things would not be said in the same way either to people in the world, or to religious living the active life. Incidentally, notice the obvious human tenderness with which St. John of the Cross writes in his letters to these nuns. It is well known that he had a special preference for this community (headed by the saintly Anne of Jesus) and he made no effort to disguise the fact that the nuns were a great consolation to him. But his love was simple and supernatural. It was not based on merely superficial considerations, but on a deep sharing of ideals and love "in the Spirit." In any case, we can see that the saint practiced what he preached and was able at the same time to love these souls who had been confided to his direction by the Lord, and to be perfectly detached in his love for them. This "reconciliation of opposites" is the mark of true sanctity. Needless to add, it gives the soul of the saint a perfectly Christ-like character, for every page of the Gospel shows us, in Christ Our Lord, a supreme harmony between well-ordered human feelings and the demands of a divine nature and personality.

All the doctrine of St. John of the Cross is aimed at this ideal balance of the human and the divine: a balance that is to be attained, however, not on a humanistic level, but "in the Spirit." Now if our human nature is to be brought under the complete and exclusive control of the Spirit of Light, then there is only one way: to follow Christ in His passion and to rise with Him from the dead. The "passion" in our life is our crucifixion by asceticism and by passive purification, especially by mystical trials. Our resurrection is the joy and the peace of contemplative prayer, and union with the Divine Spouse in mystical love.

Just as we can never separate asceticism from mysticism, so in St. John of the Cross we find darkness and light, suffering and joy, sacrifice and love united together so closely that they seem at times to be identified. It is not so much that we come through darkness to light, as that the darkness itself is light.

> Never was fount so clear, undimmed and bright;
> From it alone, I know, proceeds all light,
>   Although 'tis night.

Hence the essential simplicity of his teaching: enter into the night and you will be enlightened. "Night" means the "darkening" of all our natural desires, our natural understanding, our human way of loving; but this darkening brings with it an enlightenment. The greater our sacrifice, the deeper the night into which we plunge, the more promptly and more completely will we be enlightened. But the point to be carefully remembered is that we are *not enlightened by our own efforts, our own love, our own sacrifice*. These, on the contrary, are darkness. Even our highest spiritual abilities are darkness in the sight of God. All must be "darkened" that is to say forgotten, in order that God Himself may become the light of our soul.

The "darkness" which St. John teaches is not a pure negation. Rather it is the removal and extinguishing of a lesser light in order that pure light may shine in its place. It is like putting out a candle which is no longer of any use in the full light of day. The problem, of course, is that we *do not see* the spiritual daylight of God's presence all around us, we only see the candlelight of our own desires and judgments. This is of course familiar doctrine, common to all ascetic theologians. But one special point is emphasized by St. John of the Cross. He would extinguish not only the "light" of sensual and inordinate passions, but even certain desires, judgments and illuminations which appear to be good and holy. Indeed, he precedes by the "darkening" even of those good and helpful notions of God, those lights and consolations of prayer which have an important positive part to play in the beginnings of the spiritual life. But as we go on, if we become attached to these thoughts, ideas and images of God, and remain concerned with our selves and our spiritual progress, we will not be able to "see" the purer and more spiritual light of God Himself. Hence, as the saint says:

It is clear that, in order perfectly to attain to union in this life through grace and through love, a soul must be in darkness with respect to all that can enter through the eye, and to all that can be received through the ear, and can be imagined with the fancy, and understood with the heart, which here signifies the soul. And thus a soul is greatly impeded from reaching this high estate of union with God when it clings to any understanding or feeling or imagination or appearance or will or manner or its own, or to any other act or to anything of its own, and cannot detach and strip itself of all these. For, as we say, the goal which it seeks is beyond all this, yea, beyond even the highest thing that can be known or experienced; and thus a soul must pass beyond everything to unknowing. (Ascent of Mount Carmel, II IV, Vol. I, p. 76)

This enables us to understand the peculiar emphasis in the *Maxims* upon quietness, silence, solitude, and the "absence of business and bustle" in the interior life.

> On the road to life there is very little bustle and business, and it requires mortification of the will rather than much knowledge. He that cumbers himself least with things and pleasures will go farthest along that road. (Maxim 55)

> Since God is inaccessible, see that thou concern not thyself with how much thy faculties can comprehend and thy senses can perceive, that thou be not satisfied with less and that thy soul lose not the swiftness that is needful for one that would attain to Him. (Maxim 52)
> As one that drags a cart uphill, even so does that soul journey toward God, that shakes not off anxiety and quenches not desire. (Maxim 53)

Finally, this gives us an insight into the reason why St. John of the Cross tells his penitents to welcome darkness and spiritual trial as a great good, and assures them that when they are without consolation and light in prayer, and are fully aware of their own poverty, God is probably closer to them than ever before. Of course, this is not a universal principle for all, but it applies to those who are called to the way of contemplative prayer.

If we read the saint carefully, and take care to weigh every word, we will see that he is preaching a doctrine of pure liberty which is the very heart of the New Testament. He wants us to be free. He wants to liberate us not only from the captivity of passion and egoism, but even from the more subtle tyranny of spiritual ambition, and preoccupation with methods of prayer and systems for making progress. But of course, one must first be *called* to this contemplative freedom. The way St. John of the Cross prescribes is not fully intelligible outside of this special call to contemplative prayer. Here is what he says:

> Wherefore in this state the soul must never have meditation imposed upon it, nor must it perform any acts, nor strive after sweetness of fervor; for this would be to set an obstacle in the way of the principal agent, who . . . is God. For God secretly and quietly infuses into the soul loving knowledge and wisdom without any intervention of specific acts, although he sometimes produces them in the soul for some length of time. And the soul has then to walk in loving awareness of God, without performing specific acts, but conducting itself as we have said passively, and having no diligence of its own, but possessing this pure, simple and loving awareness, as one that opens his eyes with an awareness of love.
>
> (*Living Flame of Love* iii, 32, Vol. iii, p. 77.)

Most of the maxims and teachings collected here point to this special kind of interior peace, detachment and emptiness. St. John of the Cross strives to liberate the soul from trivial and exterior concerns, and even from lesser, more busy forms of active asceticism, in order that it may rest in detached unconcern, and yield in all simplicity to the secret action of God. The great thing is to be delivered from useless desires, desires which though they appear to be very profitable and efficacious, in reality lead us off the right road because they emphasize our own action more than the action of grace. This is St. John's main concern: that contemplatives should not waste their time and their efforts in doing work that only has to be undone by God and done over again, if they are to come to union with Him.

It is very needful, my daughters, to be able to withdraw the spirit from the devil and from sensuality, for otherwise without knowing it we shall find ourselves completely failing to make progress and very far removed from the virtues of Christ, and afterwards we shall awaken and find our work and labour inside out. Thinking that our lamp was burning, we shall find it apparently extinguished, for when we blew upon it, and thought thereby to fan its flame, we may rather have put it out.

(*Letter vi, to the nuns of Beas*)

St. John was no quietist. On the contrary few saints make more insistent demands for the right kind of work: but this work is all interior. It consists in love and suffering, not in external projects that make much noise and raise a lot of dust but, in the end, leave us no further advanced than we were before. The same letter we have just quoted insists, a few lines further down: "It is impossible to continue to make progress save by working and suffering with all virtue, *and being completely enwrapped in silence.*"

The last phrase is what is most important, and most characteristic of St. John of the Cross. It is the key to his asceticism of light in darkness, which seeks in all things to bring the soul into the *interior depths* where love is invisible, and to rescue it from the triviality of the obvious and showy forms of spiritual life which are good only for those who remain on the surface.

Any one of the maxims of St. John of the Cross is an inexhaustible mine of spiritual truth for the reader who really, sincerely and humbly seeks to renounce himself and abandon himself, in faith, to the mercy of God.

The ascetic teaching of St. John of the Cross is part and parcel of his mysticism and cannot be separated from it. That is why the poems of St. John happily complete the aphorisms and cautions, and incite the reader to go on to the saint's great mystical treatises which are nothing but commentaries on his poems. The remarkable beauty of his poems shows that his asceticism, far from destroying his creative genius, had liberated and transformed it by dedicating it to God.

THE PRIMITIVE
CARMELITE IDEAL

1 . *The prophetic spirit*

When we approach the question of the origins of the Carmelite Order and of its primitive spirituality, we must first
of all make a clear-cut distinction between this new form of
life and the ancient monastic tradition of the west. If we
make the mistake that has been made by some historians
and view the Carmelites as another expression of the same
movement of monastic renewal that brought into being the
Camaldolese, the Cistercians, the Carthusians, the Vallom-
brosans, the Grandmontines and so many others in the 11th
and 12th centuries, we will be doomed to confusion and
ambiguity from the start. We will be forced to explain what
cannot be explained: the evolution of a monastic order into
an order of mendicant preaching friars.

The problem is actually far more subtle. The first Carmelites had initiated something quite original and unique:
a loose-knit community of hermits with an informal, occa-

sional apostolate. Neither the eremitical nor the apostolic aspects of this new life were systematically organized and neither was the subject of a formal program such as we would envisage at the present time, when starting "something new." But the fact is, that in abandoning this original plan and conforming to the successful and more highly organized institution of the mendicants, with a special apostolic purpose, the Carmelites of the second generation had perhaps let go of something quite unique and quite characteristically their own, in order to follow something that was successfully working, but had been devised by others for a considerably different purpose. It remains open to question, of course, to what extent the originality of the first Carmelites was lost in the process of this transformation. To say that it disappeared altogether would not fit the facts. But to say that it was considerably modified is only to bring to mind the source of the contentions and divisions which plagued the early history of the Order.

The Carmelites were originally hermits. And of course their life was the traditional hermit life known to the east from the earliest centuries of the Church. They lived as the desert fathers had lived eight hundred years earlier. They began as an offshoot of the ancient, informal, charismatic monachism of Syria and Palestine. But they were not monks in the western sense, and they never were. They were originally not cenobites. They had no liturgical office in common. They did not live in monasteries or cloisters. They were in fact simple laymen, living as solitaries in a loosely connected group, in caves and huts on the side of Mount Carmel. Their manner of life was not yet institutionalized, and even when they first asked for a Rule, from the hands of the Patriarch of Jerusalem, that Rule was, as we shall see, deliberately kept simple and uncomplicated. Its formal prescriptions were left at the bare minimum. There was just enough "legislation" to preserve the primitive simplicity and purpose of the life. What was that purpose? In the words of the Rule itself, it was: "Let each one remain in his cell or near it, meditating day and night on the Law of the Lord, and vigilant in prayer, unless he is legitimately occupied in something else."

Nothing could be simpler. The purpose of the life was solitude and contemplation, but within a framework that allowed complete liberty for the individual development of each one under the guidance of the Holy Spirit. It was a kind of informal "lay-monasticism" of a solitary type. To say that meditative prayer came first of all was to make clear that contemplation was the primary and indeed the unique purpose of the life. But at the same time it was not to be considered as something that rigidly excluded every other activity whatever. On the contrary, room was left for other legitimate activities, within due proportion. And apparently, even at the very beginning, a certain apostolate was conceded to be a normal and legitimate overflow from this life of prayer. Of course this apostolate would be extremely restricted. It would undoubtedly be a matter less of preaching than of other works of mercy since only a few of the hermits were priests. Yet preaching was most certainly included in the Carmelite life even in its earliest beginnings. What is important however is not the fact that preaching was considered part of the life, but that the life itself was left free and informal so that the hermits could do anything that conformed to their ideal of solitude and free submission to the Holy Spirit. The primitive Carmelites could preach, as they could also engage in any other work of mercy. What were the conditions? We would say today, these works were legitimate as long as they remained subordinate to a life of contemplation. But this abstract formula is itself misleading. To put it more concretely, they could do whatever good work was compatible with a life of which most was spent in the solitude of the cell, meditating on the Law of the Lord.

Even the inexorable defender of solitude and opponent of the life led by Carmelites in the cities of the west, the General of the Order called Nicholas the Frenchman, admitted willingly that the preaching apostolate was an integral part of the purest and most primitive tradition of the Order, the tradition which he himself defended. But it had to be an apostolate of solitaries and contemplatives, not of friars living in a busy city. He wrote:

> Conscious of their imperfection, the hermits of Carmel persevered for a long time in the solitude of the desert, but as they intended to be of service to their neighbor, in order not to be guilty of infidelity to their way, they went sometimes, but rarely, down from their hermitage. That which they had harvested with the sickle of contemplation, in solitude, they went to thresh it on the threshing floor of preaching, and to sow it abroad on all sides.[1]

What is the explanation of this? It is probably to be sought in the symbolic adoption by the Carmelites of the prophet Elias as their "Founder." It is quite true that the hermits living on the slopes of Mount Carmel, near the "spring of Elias," where the prophet himself had prayed and dwelt alone, and where the "sons of the prophets" had

[1] From the French translation of the ancient text known as the *Ignea Sagitta* (Burning Arrow) in *Les Plus Vieux Textes du Carmel*, Paris 1944, p. 173.

had a "school," [2] could themselves claim to be descendants of the ancient prophets. It is quite true that Elias, in a broad sense, was the "founder" of this way of life since he had in fact been the inspiration of those countless generations that had lived there in the places hallowed by his memory and stamped with his indelible character.

The first Carmelites then were not only hermits and descendants of the early desert fathers, but they were also very conscious of a certain *prophetic* character about their vocation. This meant of course that they were inclined to give precedence to what we would call the "mystical" side of their vocation over the ascetic, never of course neglecting or excluding the latter. For in the truly contemplative life, contemplation and asceticism necessarily go hand in hand. You cannot really have the first without the second, though it is not impossible for a monastic life to consist of asceticism without contemplation, except in a formal and exterior sense of the word.

A prophet in the traditional sense is not merely a man who foretells the future under spiritual inspiration. That is in fact quite accidental. He is above all a "witness," just as the martyr is a witness. (The Greek word martyr means witness.) But he is a witness in a different way than the martyr. The martyr suffers death. The prophet suffers inspiration, or vision. He shoulders the "burden" of vision that God lays upon him. He bows under the truth and the judgments of God, sometimes the concrete, definite historical judgment pronounced on a given age, sometimes only the manifestation of God's transcendent and secret holiness, which is denied and opposed by sin in general.

[2] *Schola* not only in the sense of a place where one learns, but in the more original and etymological sense of a place of leisure, quiet and retirement, where one can think deeply.

But above all the prophet is one who bears the burden of the divine mercy—a burden which is a gift to mankind, but which remains a burden to the prophet in so far as no one will take it from him. In this connection, we can see that St. Therese of Lisieux was a true descendant of the early, prophetic saints of her Order when she took upon herself the burden of victimhood of the merciful love of God. This consecration of our modern saint is not fully understandable unless it is seen in the light of the early prophetic tradition of Carmel. In fact, she realized this ideal most perfectly in herself, and for that reason she became in our time the patroness of the Catholic missions. For the missionary too needs to realize that he is a prophet bearing a burden, a burden of mercy and of truth which too often men are unable to receive. He is not merely an official, or a teacher, who comes to organize a Christian community and to disseminate doctrinal truths. He bears with him, in his sacramental power, not merely news about Christ, but the presence of the Redeemer and the fact of Redemption.

If we are to understand the true notion of the prophetic spirit which Carmel concretized around the symbolic figure of Elias, we must recall to mind all the meaning of the prophetic vocation in Old Testament times. A prophet is one who lives in direct submission to the Holy Spirit in order that, by his life, actions and words, he may at all times be a sign of God in the world of men. Christ the Incarnate Word was of course the supreme Prophet, and all sanctity participates in this prophetic quality. Their submission to God is not merely a matter of charismatic accident but of perfect fidelity to grace.

The prophet is a man of God not only in the sense that he is seized and controlled passively by God, but much more truly in the sense that he is consciously and freely obedient to the Holy Spirit, no matter what the price may be. And this presupposes fidelity in all the obscure mysterious trials by which his soul is purified so that he may become a divine instrument. The great prophets of Israel were men of God, divine instruments, whose function it was to keep alive the spirit of equality, theocratic independence and spiritual autonomy which had characterized the life of Israel in the desert. The Lord had liberated Israel "with a strong arm" from Egypt that they "might sacrifice to Him in the desert." (Exodus 5: 1-4) This was necessary for several reasons: not only that Israel might be free to follow a special and divine call, but also because God would not accept, from His people, a sacrifice consisting of the "abomination" of the Egyptians. It was not His plan that Israel should simply resign itself to slavery under Pharaoh with its hardships and "offer up" the toil of making bricks without straw, thereby giving an example of virtue to the Egyptians!

The forty years in the desert came to be regarded as the golden age of the history of Israel, the age of Israel's nuptials with the Lord—the pattern of all future perfection. For after settling in the Promised Land, Israel was tempted to leave the austere, unseen yet ever-present and all merciful Lord of the desert, and ally herself in adulterous union with the visible, dramatic and sometimes licentious gods of the fertile Canaanite land. She would be recalled to order by the prophets, and always in the same terms: return to the spirit of your days in the desert! Recovery of the spirit of the desert meant a return to fidelity, to charity, to fraternal union; it meant the destruction of the inequalities and oppressions dividing rich and poor; conversion to justice and equity meant the return to the true sabbath. For the law of the desert was the law of the sabbath, of peace, direct dependence on the Lord, silence and trust, forgiveness of debts, restoration of unity, purity of worship. This spiritual sabbath had been corrupted by the levitical jurists into a vast complex of legalistic problems and moral cases. The prophets, like Isaias inveighed against this perversion of the true spirit. Always, with Osee, they summoned Israel back to the fidelity of the desert. "Behold I will allure her" says Yaweh to Osee, "and lead her into the wilderness, and will speak to her heart." (Osee 2:14) In the days of King Achab, when Jezabel the queen was filling the land with priests of Baal, Yaweh raised up His prophet Elias as a witness and a messenger to Israel. The first public act of the prophet was to declare that there would be a three years' drought, a symbolic punishment and purification—a reminder of the desert.

> And Elias the Thesbite of the inhabitants of Galaad said to Achab: as the Lord liveth, in whose sight I stand, there shall not be dew nor rain these years but according to the words of my mouth.
>
> (3 Kings, 17:1)

The early Carmelite Fathers read much meaning into these words of the prophets and into their context, finding here an allegory of the whole Carmelite vocation. To stand in the presence of the living God, first of all. Then to "go toward the east and hide thyself in the torrent of Carith . . . and there thou shalt drink of the torrent: and I have commanded ravens to feed thee there." (id. 3-4)

The author of that moving ancient text on the spirit of Carmelite prayer and contemplation, the *Institution* of the first Fathers, interprets the retirement of Elias in typical medieval style. To hide in the torrent of Carith is to embrace the ascetical life, which leads to the perfection of charity by one's own efforts, aided by the grace of God. To drink of the

torrent is to passively receive the secret light of contemplation from God and to be inwardly transformed by His
wisdom:

> . . . to taste, in a certain manner, in our heart, and to experi-
> ence in our spirit the power of the divine presence and the
> sweetness of the glory from on high, not only after death but
> even in this mortal life. That is what is really meant by drink-
> ing from the torrent of the joy of God . . . It is in order to
> accomplish this twofold end (asceticism and contemplation)
> that the monk must enter upon the eremitical way, accord-
> ing to the testimony of the prophet: "In a desert land, where
> there is no way, and no water so in the sanctuary have I come
> before thee, to see thy power and thy glory." [3]

The Carmelite, then, is the successor of the prophets as
witness to the desert vocation of Israel, that is of the
Church: a reminder that we do not have on this earth a
lasting city, and that we are pilgrims to the city of God.
But, more specifically, the Carmelite seeks, by his preaching
and by the witness of his contemplative life, not merely to
bring the Gospel message to the people at large, but above
all, and in a special way, to lead others in the ways of prayer,
contemplation and solitude. The Carmelite Apostolate has,
ideally speaking, this very special modality of its own. It is
a contemplative apostolate to other potential contemplatives. It is an apostolate of interior prayer. It is a "school of
prophets." It teaches, indeed, but what it teaches above all
is the way of the hidden life. And here above all, *nemo dat
quod non habet*. No one can give something which he does
not himself have.

[3] *Les Plus Vieux Textes*, p. 114. The *Institution* is by an unknown
author, probably of the 14 century. The Biblical quote is from Psalm
62:3.

If Elias stands as the model of all Carmelites, there is another and more ideal figure than that of the prophet: the figure of the Blessed Virgin of Mount Carmel who, even more than Elias, embodies in herself the perfection of the Carmelite ideal. Where in Elias we see at once the zeal and the weaknesses of the prophet, his greatness and his imperfections, his conflicts and inner contradictions, in Mary we see a sanctity that is beyond prophecy and beyond conflict, hidden in perfect humility and in ordinariness. It would therefore be a tragic mistake to look at the Carmelite ideal too exclusively from the prophetic viewpoint. This would lead to distortion and dramatization, to violence and ultimately to a kind of pharisaical pretense. But the example and influence of the Queen of prophets are there to heal these divisions. The sanctity of Our Lady was great indeed, but so great that it cannot adequately be expressed in anything other than the ordinary ways of human existence. In this, as in so many other things, she resembles her Divine Son. Like Him, she was in all things human and ordinary, close to her fellow men, simple and unassuming in her way of life, without drama and without exaltation. The true, sure instinct of the Carmelite saints has gone direct to the heart of this truth. The mysticism of St. Theresa is rooted in a life of ordinariness and common sense, because it accepts the wholeness of human nature just as it is. The doctrine of St. John of the Cross goes to the greatest lengths to exclude everything that savors of heroic show and mystical display, discarding all visions, revelations, locutions and ecstasies in favor of "dark faith." For "in order for the understanding to be prepared for divine union, it must be pure and void of all that pertains to sense, and detached and freed from all that can clearly be perceived by the understanding, profoundly hushed and put to silence, and leaning upon faith which

alone is the proximate and proportionate means whereby
the soul is united to God." [4]

The "little way" of St. Therese of Lisieux is predominantly
a Marian way. The whole spirit and ideal of Carmel is, at
least implicitly, a re-living of that great mystery of faith in
the Blessed Virgin who was "blessed because she believed"
(Luke 1:45) and who, by her faith, brought the Lord of
Majesty into the world in human form.

It can be said that the Carmelite spirit is essentially a
"desert" spirit, a prophetic ideal. And that Elias represents
the exterior, the more material aspect of that ideal. But
that the Virgin Mary is the symbol and source of the interior
spirit of Carmel. Which means that in the long run, the desert spirit and prophetic ideal of Carmel are understood most
perfectly by those who have entered into the "dark night"
of Marian faith.

II . *Carmelite origins*

Who were the first Carmelites? It would be very interesting
to know more about them. They were pilgrims and Crusaders from the west who, in the 12th century, renounced
the world with its ambitions and its wars—even its "holy
wars"—in order to consecrate their lives to God in solitude
on Mount Carmel. The first Carmelites were men whom
the spirit of Elias had rescued from the awful shipwreck that
was the second Crusade, preached by St. Bernard of Clairvaux. They were men who had been launched into war by a
cenobite, the holiest and greatest prophet of their time. It
is certain that Bernard himself must first have communi-

. [4] Ascent of Mount Carmel, Bk. ii, c. 9, vol. i. (Peers trans.) p. 98.

cated to them something of that spirit and power of Elias, the burning and shining light that was in him.

A Greek monk, John Phocas, on pilgrimage to the Holy Land, gives the following description of the westerners living as hermits on Carmel. The text, written about 1185, undoubtedly refers to events going back ten or twenty years before the writing.

> At the end of the point that looks out over the sea, we find the cave of the prophet Elias. This extraordinary man there lived an altogether angelic life, before being taken up into heaven. In this place there was once a big building whose ruins are still there today . . . For some time, now, a white-haired monk, invested with the priestly dignity and a native of Calabria, has made his dwelling in the ruins of this monastery, as a result of a vision in which the prophet Elias appeared to him; he has built a little wall and a tower, with a chapel, and about ten brethren have gathered about him. He is living there still today.[5]

It is thought by some historians that this hermit was not a Calabrian, but a Frenchman, St. Berthold of Malifay, a native of the Limousin in west-central France. He was the predecessor of Saint Brocard, generally considered the founder of the Order as he received the rule from the Patriarch.

The "Rule of St. Albert" as the primitive Carmelite legislation is called, was not written by a Carmelite at all. The original hermits, laymen gathered around one or two simple priests, felt that they ought to receive some definite code of life from the Church. They applied to the Patriarch of Jerusalem, Albert of Avogardo, an Augustinian canon. This prelate, with great discretion, drew up a simple set of monastic usages covering the essentials of the solitary life. To

[5] Les Plus Vieux Textes p. 59.

give them a firm and reliable structure, he had them elect a
Prior whom they would obey, traced out the broad lines of
their life of poverty in solitude, reminding them of their
chief obligation: to spend their days in solitary prayer, working and praying alone in their cells.

In the preamble to this rule, St. Albert recalled to their
minds that all religious life is first and foremost the service
of the Lord and "dependence on Jesus Christ, serving Him
faithfully with a pure heart and a good conscience." A simple and seemingly obvious sentence, which nevertheless
contains in it the principles of a truly interior and spiritual
life of prayer. Without such a spirit as this, no life at all,
however contemplative, however sacrificial, has any deep
Christian significance.

It also goes without saying that, like every other form of
Christian ascetical life, the life of the hermits of Mount Carmel was above all a life of charity, of fraternal unity in
Christ. Not of course that it was cenobitic: but the hermits
too, though, solitaries, lived in deep spiritual communion
and fraternal solidarity with one another. When, later, Nicholas the Frenchman so vehemently lamented what he
thought was the decline of the Order, when the Carmelites
moved to western Europe and began to live in cities, he
did this not only because they had apparently lost their ideal
of solitude, but also because it seemed to him that they were
losing their charity and their union in Christ. And it is true
that the crisis of adaptation to life in the west as mendicants did severely threaten the original unity of the Order.

Few facts are known about the early history of the Carmelites in the east. In 1187, after the defeat of the Christian
armies, St. Berthold built a monastery near the fountain of
Elias. This was not a step towards the common life, but
rather a way of providing a refuge for the hermits in case of

attack. However the Carmelites did have establishments even in towns, at this early date. They maintained a hospice in Jerusalem, a chapel at Sareptha (presumably for pilgrims), a monastery at Acre and another in the city of Tyre. They also had a monastery called Beaulieu, on Mount Lebanon. There were other eremitical colonies of Carmelites including one across the Jordan on the Mountain of the Forty Days' Fast.

At first the Carmelites were not troubled by the Saracens. The more remote colonies of hermits were however devastated in 1240. Already in 1238, a group of hermits had taken refuge in Cyprus, another in Sicily, while a third was established at Les Aygalades, near Marseilles. In 1241 some Carmelites went to England, and St. Louis, visiting the holy mountain in 1254, took six of them with him to Paris. After the fall of Acre in 1291, the last Carmelites in the east were exterminated. They died, we are told, singing the *Salve Regina*.

The fact that the Carmelites moved west in small groups, and settled in places distant from one another, in divergent situations, meant that the unity of the Order was gravely threatened from the very start. What is surprising is not the fact that history of the Order now became a long series of misunderstandings and divisions, but rather the fact that it survived at all. In brief, the source of the trouble was this: those who led the way to Europe, though they at first settled in out of the way places, also began to live in towns and to engage in the active apostolate. They met with great opposition, particularly on the part of the secular clergy. But they were convinced that the only way in which they could gain a solid footing in the west and thus perpetuate the Order, was to present themselves as Mendicant Friars like the Dominicans and Franciscans.

In 1265, when Nicholas the Frenchman came west from Carmel to attend the General Chapter of the Order,—at which he was elected Prior General to succeed St. Simon Stock—he found this situation which was to him incomprehensible and deeply disturbing. Unable to change matters, he denounced the trend away from solitude and retired to a hermitage, as we shall see in detail.

St. Simon Stock is mainly credited for the transformation of the Order of Mount Carmel into a mendicant and apostolic institute. In order to do this, he caused the Rule to be revised by two Dominicans and moved the brethren into towns and cities, laying a strong emphasis on the common life. The Order then became divided between isolated houses where the hermit life still continued in force, and town houses where the common life was the rule and everyone was engaged in apostolic work. In order to form priests and apostles, houses of study were of course necessary. Hence the Carmelites founded in university cities, such as Cambridge (1249), Oxford (1253), Paris (1259) and Bologna (1260). In addition, each province had its own *studium generale*.

To what extent was St. Simon Stock the savior of the Carmelite Order? Would the Order have survived without this transformation? If it had remained a small coterie of hermits, would its destinies have been less flourishing? It is impossible to answer these questions, but the debate is by no means finished. In the eyes of the saint's immediate successors, the change had been a fatal mistake which could only be repaired by a complete return to solitude. But such a return was no longer possible. There are not lacking writers today who believe that the abandonment of the hermit life was the end of the genuine Carmelite ideal. Others, representing a more common opinion, like Fr Bruno de Jesus

Marie, prefer the view that only in Europe did Carmel find its true stature and identity, in the union of contemplation and the apostolate. Whatever the true answer may be (if a true answer can be found at all) the difficulties encountered by the nascent Order were truly enormous.

As anyone familiar with thirteenth century history realizes, the mendicants were thought by conventional minds to be turning the Church of God upside down. Their advent was regarded by the "old fashioned" as a dangerous revolution. In such circumstances, the appearance of yet another new and unconventional group could only increase the confusion and unrest. The Carmelite friars were forced to find themselves a recognizable place in the Church of their time: they had to belong to some category before they could be comfortably dealt with by anxious canonists. There was no need of a new monastic Order—or they could have become another group of hermits like the Carthusians or Camaldolese. However, there seemed to be a better reason why they should turn toward the mendicants. Not only did these Orders correspond with the most vital needs of the Church in the thirteenth century, but also Carmel itself had as one of its integral notes, the need of an apostolic outlet for the overflow of contemplation.

But for the Carmelite friar, it was not, as for the Dominican, a matter of a special vocation to preach the Gospel,—that is to say, the apostolate was not the main end of the Carmelite vocation. On the other hand, since contemplation was the main end of the life, it followed that the sharing of the fruits of contemplation was a secondary end, inseparable from the first. This was a new approach to the apostolic life, a development that had not been suspected in the old monastic setup, except in individual cases like those of St. Gregory the Great and St. Bernard of Clairvaux who were so to speak the exception to the rule, and as such were very articulate in bewailing their fate. For them it *was against the nature of their vocation* to be called to the apostolate. A paradoxical exception permitted by the inscrutable designs of God. But for the new thirteenth century mentality, explicitly formulated by St. Thomas Aquinas, an apostolate of preaching became on the contrary the ordinary outcome of perfect contemplation.

Not all the Carmelites accepted this spontaneously and without reserves. On the contrary, it was quite natural that the conservative, eremitical group should regard it with the same eyes as a Benedictine, a Cistercian or a Carthusian of that time.

The primitive Rule of St. Albert had been approved by the Holy See in 1226. But now that the Carmelites were in the west, and were beginning to see that their place was among the mendicant Orders, the Rule had to be revised. St. Simon Stock here called upon the aid of two Dominicans, Hugh of St. Cher and William of Antera. These two adjusted the primitive Rule with certain subtle, accidental changes which nevertheless made it possible for the whole life and outlook of Carmel to be completely transformed. In a word, the changes in the Rule resulted in a reorientation of the Carmelite life in the direction of apostolic activity, without however altering the basic obligation for the friars to be, before all else, contemplatives.

In brief, the changes introduced by the Dominican revisers of the Rule, in cooperation with St. Simon Stock and the western Superiors of the Order, were these:

1) Where there had only been a vow of obedience, now the vows of chastity and poverty became explicit. This was nothing new in itself, only a canonical step to put the Car-

melites on the same juridical footing as the other mendicants.

2) It was now made clear that the friars could live "anywhere suitable" which meant that they could live in towns, in order to engage in the apostolate. This was a radical departure from the primitive eremitical concept, and it was considered by many in the Order to be unacceptable. But in fact the Popes began to demand that this change be made. John XXII moved ten Carmelite communities from solitude into cities in order that they might more effectively carry on the apostolate.

3) Whereas in the first version of the Rule each one kept to his cell, and not even the divine office was recited in common, there now came to be a greater emphasis on the common life and common exercises. Meals, for instance, were to be taken in common. At the same time, the rules for fasting and abstinence were slackened, and meat was permitted at certain times.

4) The rules of silence were also mitigated.

5) Finally, the poverty of the Order was given a strictly mendicant character. It was stipulated that the Friars could not own land but that they could have certain domestic animals, including mules to ride on. This implied travel.

These changes were incorporated into the Rule and became part of the primitive Rule of St. Albert. And it was to this Rule, modified in 1247 by St. Simon Stock and the two Dominicans, that St. Theresa was to return in her reform. Hence, in practical fact, the primitive Carmelite ideal is embodied in the Rule as adapted for the apostolate in the west, and not in the original, purely eremitical Rule first drawn up by the Patriarch, even though that allowed, implicitly, certain excursions into the apostolate. The struggle over the primitive Rule in 16th century Spain was, then, a struggle for the Rule as adapted in 1247 against another greatly relaxed version of the Rule which was put into effect in 1413 and which the Calced Carmelites followed, in opposition to St. Theresa's reform.

Nevertheless, in the thirteenth century there was a pronounced reaction in favor of the earlier, more eremitical ideal of the Order, led above all by Nicholas the Frenchman. And in the sixteenth century, within the Discalced Reform, there was also an extreme wing which sought solitude along with austerity and centralization: and this was the faction of Doria and the Friars of Pastrana, who eventually persecuted St. John of the Cross, and hounded him to his death. The curious thing is that St. John of the Cross, the defender of the pure Carmelite ideal of mystical contemplation, was himself not an extremist in favor of pure solitude, nor did he advocate extreme austerity, but took the middle way, favoring the combination of solitude, and contemplation with preaching and the direction of souls.

Hence it is evident that in the history of the Carmelites the pure and primitive spirit of the Order always remains incarnate in a kind of "prophetic" union of solitude and apostolate. When this balance is disturbed, when the shift is made too far in one direction or the other, then the primitive spirit is lost. That is to say that when too much emphasis is placed on apostolic action, the primitive spirit is of course weakened and eventually destroyed. But that does not mean that the return to the original ideal is a mere matter of abandoning the apostolate and embracing a solitary life that is primarily ascetical and austere. It seems likely that the apostolate, when kept in its right place, *remains the true guarantee* of the original purity of the ideal. For a Carmelite, the apostolate in its own way encourages contemplation, just as con-

templation is the source of a genuine apostolate. To abandon
the apostolate altogether in what we might call a kind of
"left wing deviation" would result not in a purification of the
contemplative spirit, but rather its stultification in the rigidity
of an artificial, formalistic cult of solitude and asceticism for
their own sakes. This at any rate appears to be the lesson of
Carmelite history, both in the 13th century and, more particularly, in the 16th. The problem was very successfully solved
by St. John of the Cross and by those who, following him,
remained true to the genial and inspired intuitions of St.
Theresa of Avila.

III . *The Fiery Arrow*

What has just been said is no more than an opinion, a ten-
tative judgment, which however seems to be the commonly
accepted view among Carmelite theologians. But once the
judgment has been made, we must face the provoking witness of that "prophetic" successor of St. Simon Stock: I
mean the author of *The Fiery Arrow*, Nicholas the Frenchman.

The *Fiery Arrow*, is, for very good reasons, little known.
One of the most urgent, most passionate of all the docu-
ments in a long literary history of contemplative religion, it
is so outspoken that it has rarely, if ever, been printed in its
entirety. It has not even been made known, except in frag-
mentary fashion, in the Carmelite Order itself. Even today,
the *Ignea Sagitta* has been published only in part. The French
translation (published in 1944) soon went out of print and
as far as I know is no longer available. It is still quite likely
that the *Fiery Arrow* is completely unknown to many members of the Carmelite Order. But in discussing the primitive

ideal of Carmel, such a document can hardly be left out of the account. It must be considered with care.

It would of course be interesting to speculate on the reasons for the long-standing neglect of an important document. But that is a delicate question, and should not after all be brought by anyone who is not professionally concerned with Carmelite history. The outside observer may content himself with remarking that this seems to be another manifestation of something almost universal in religious history. Once an institution has been set up and is successfully running, anything that calls into question its validity, its authenticity or the quality of its achievement is feared and resented: not necessarily out of base motives, but for solid, though perhaps expedient reasons. It is always felt that once a stable situation has been reached, and problems have been to some extent solved, it is better not to cause unrest, to re-open old wounds, and needlessly to excite the aspirations of the members with reminders of some other ideal. This is especially true wherever there is question of some opposition between community life and life in solitude.

In the case of the *Fiery Arrow*, the author speaks with a fervor, a conviction and even a certain asperity of accusation which would scarcely admit of compromising acceptance. Those who could not receive all his arguments with favor would almost necessarily reject everything. For our own part, however, looking at the work objectively and free from administrative concern, we feel it is permitted to admire the author and sympathize with his ideals. Even admitting that he has missed the target in placing too exclusive an emphasis on solitude, it is permitted to feel that he has nevertheless spoken with the authentic voice of the first Carmelites, and that his witness is not to be rejected without serious consideration. Indeed, if he is accepted, he may have very much to contribute to the modern and current teaching that the Carmelite vocation is both contemplative and apostolic. This is something that the *Fiery Arrow* also asserts with explicit clarity. Its only complaint is that in aligning itself with the mendicants, the Carmelite Order sacrificed its own true and unique originality as an order of apostolic hermits.

It is all important to understand clearly the historical situation in which the *Fiery Arrow* was written. The first groups had left Carmel and had been in the west for some thirty years when Nicholas, a hermit who had come direct from Carmel, was elected Prior General. The religious community he took over from St. Simon Stock was to him completely unrecognizable. The Rule had been rewritten by Dominicans, and the Friars were building convents in cities, acting in practice as if their Order had been founded "in order to preach." It is true that there is something about the *Fiery Arrow* which suggests the violent anti-mendicant pamphlets of the time, like those of William of Saint Amour, refuted by St. Thomas Aquinas. It is possible that Nicholas was instinctively ultra-conservative and that he was shocked by the whole mendicant movement. But this fact is not enough to explain his vehement indignation against the Carmelite apostles. He was not simply inveighing against the apostolic life. Far from it. What seemed to him to be a scandal and a decline equal to the tragedy mourned by Jeremias in the Lamentations was the fact that men called to be hermits, men without sufficient preparation, without study, without discipline and without regular safeguards, were playing at the full-time apostolic life without having a sufficient appreciation of its responsibilities and burdens. Anyone who is intimately acquainted with communities of contemplatives can well understand with what concern a superior might see them suddenly precipitated into the active ministry.

The Carmelite Order was really in a state of grave crisis. The transition from east to west and from contemplation to apostolate had been too rapid. The Carmelites had not yet sunk deep roots in their new homes. Numerous postulants were entering, but their motives for entering were confused since the Superiors themselves were still disoriented. It is said that large numbers of the older members were leaving to join the established monastic Orders, while the younger ones, preferring to be frankly active, were attracted to the Franciscans and Dominicans. There were of course newly founded houses of study for Carmelites in the university cities. But these were not yet well established, and the level of doctrinal formation was as yet probably not very high. Furthermore, as Carmelite historians tell us[6] that academic degrees brought with them exemptions and privileges and this meant that there was a rush for doctorates that was not entirely based on zeal for theological science and for the apostolate, but on more human reasons as well. This was made worse by the fact that doctorates could be acquired by indult from Rome dispensing from the necessary studies. Such men were *doctores bullati*. In these circumstances it was natural that a contemplative like Nicholas should react energetically. In the presence of this dangerous situation, Nicholas had only one answer. His solution was naturally the only one he would be likely to think of: return to the desert! Live in Europe as you lived in the east. Live as you lived on Carmel. In this way he hoped to clarify the situation and salvage the originality of a hermit life with a very restricted and occasional apostolate.

From many points of view he was right. Yet facts and the

[6] Fr. Benedict Zimmerman, article "Carmes" in the *Dictionnaire de Théologie Catholique*.

decision of the Church were to contradict him. The Council of Lyons, in 1274, definitely ranked the Carmelites among mendicant and preaching Orders. The judgment of history upon the *Fiery Arrow* seems to be that, if Nicholas had been followed, the Carmelite Order would perhaps have had an ephemeral existence and would have died out with the thirteenth century. It would perhaps never have fulfilled its providential mission to contemplate and to share the fruits of contemplation in that very special way characteristic of it: by the formation and direction of interior souls in other orders and in the world.

Yet here is another case where a man who may in some sense have been proved pragmatically wrong by history, still remains as a noble witness not to a lost cause but to an undying truth: and the truth which, in the practical order, Nicholas was unable to defend in his own way, remains ideally speaking fundamental to the Carmelite spirit. It would be a serious mistake to regard Nicholas as a pathological crank. If he has been passed over in silence, it is not because he was a violent and deluded figure, but perhaps rather because his witness is too pure and too uncompromising to be accepted without confusion by generations unused to primitive simplicity. There is no reason why we should not pay attention to him, and be inspired by him, as long as we recognize at the same time that he must not be called upon to justify irresponsible and immature gestures of reformism, which do not take account of historical fact.

His modern editor, Pere Francois de Sainte Marie, O.C.D., sums up his case fairly and well:

Nicholas is not a tyrannical defender of solitude, nor a conservative clinging literally to the observance in which he himself was formed, he is simply an authentic contemplative, endowed with a keen sense of the mystery and of the exigencies of contemplation.[7]

We wonder if perhaps even more could be said for him than this: that he was not only an authentic contemplative, convinced by experience, of the beauties and nobility of the contemplative life, but that he was, above all, one who fully realized the implications of the early Carmelite ideal in all its originality and uniqueness: the ideal of a "prophetic" eremitism, in which solitude was essential and all important, but in which from time to time, as the Holy Ghost inspired or as occasion might demand, there was need for a brief and apostolic witness, perhaps only to a few isolated souls. What Nicholas opposed was not the apostolate, but a mass apostolate, on a large scale, with the need for much study and continuous preaching in towns.

In other words, Nicholas was, paradoxically, a representative of the pure and prophetic spirit of the early Carmelites, even though he appeared to be "prophetically" wrong. If we were to evaluate him by the kind of standard used by Marxists, we would simply say that he had judged wrongly and that his judgment was discarded by history, which he had not "interpreted correctly." As Catholics, though we may respect pragmatic judgments in historical matters, we owe loyalty to certain truths that are eternally valid. What Nicholas had to say as prophet and as contemplative cannot be discarded by history. It has meaning for contemplatives in every age. But it has a special meaning for Carmelites. He is then "prophetic" after all in the sense that he clearly enunciated what was essential and "Elianic" in the Carmelite ideal: the primacy of solitude and contemplation, not "in spite of" or

[7] *Les Plus Vieux Textes,* p. 161.

"against" apostolic work, but even for the sake of an apostolate that would be all the more effective on account of its
restricted, occasional and even quasi-charismatic character.

In summary, the *Fiery Arrow* written as an encyclical to
the Carmelite Order when Nicholas was giving up his office
in disgust, is partly an earnest exhortation to return to the
pure spirit of the Rule of St. Albert, and partly a commen-
tary on the essential prescriptions of that Rule. In the mind
of Nicholas the Frenchman, the Carmelites who were living
in towns and attempting to preach the Gospel on a large
scale without sufficient authority or preparation, were unfaithful to their vocation, were dividing and destroying their
Order, and were accomplishing nothing of any pastoral
value, that might justify or excuse their defection. They were
losing their own souls without helping the souls of others.
The reason for this, he thought, was not merely the physical
fact that they lived in towns rather than in the forests, but
rather that they had abandoned their ideal of prayer, solitude and charity. Let us hear his own words:

As long as the brethren were united, bound together by sincere charity, and refused to violate their promises; as long as
they remained in their cells instead of running about the world,
as long as they meditated on the Law of the Lord and were
vigilant in prayer, not out of obligation alone but because they
were inspired by the impulsion of spiritual joy, as long as they
persevered in this gladness, they were true sons (of Carmel).
But disunity and inconstancy have split wide open the cement
of charity and the stones of the sanctuary have been scattered
to the four corners of the world. (p. 167)

Did not the Lord our Savior grant us the favor of leading us
into solitude, and speaking familiarly to our hearts, He who
does not manifest Himself to His friends in public, in the

noise of the streets, but in intimacy, by the grace of spiritual
joy, in order to reveal to them His mysteries and His secrets?
Be not then like mules! Do not imagine that the Lord speaks
with fools who seek their own enjoyment or the pleasure of
their senses in the vanity of this world, among the crowd of
men given to vice, or in the chaos of sinful thoughts that separate a man from God: He wishes, on the contrary, that each
one may guard his heart in honor and sanctity, pure of all sin
and far from all danger of it. Without mentioning the disgust
which such profound stupidity inspires, I ask myself with as-
tonishment why you have chosen the consolation of the world.
You cannot possess the joy of God and the joy of this world
at the same time. They do not go together, they cannot be
reconciled. (p. 171)

It is easy to recognize in this passage the basic principles
familiar to every reader of St. John of the Cross, particularly
those with which he opens his *Ascent of Mount Carmel*.
Nicholas the Frenchman was unable, unfortunately, to
quote from the Carmelite Doctor of the Church who came
only three centuries after him. Instead, he quoted another
who had lived and preached a century before, St. Bernard
of Clairvaux: "Divine joy is a delicate thing which is not
given to one who seeks any other."

The important thing about this passage is the directness
and clarity with which Nicholas attacks, not the apostolic
life but simply the sensuality and inconstancy of contemplatives who have grown tired of solitude or have never learned
to love it. Anyone can see that this is a vastly different
matter. An apostolate that is merely an evasion of a more urgent and more personal responsibility is valueless before God
and man. It is nothing but self-delusion, and cannot claim
to be based on genuine charity. It can no longer be said

with certainty to what extent Nicholas was fair in his judgment of his contemporaries, particularly of that restless younger generation which had not enjoyed the advantages he himself had enjoyed in the east. Doubtless there were shiftless and undisciplined men among them. But history has shown that the majority must have been worth more than the impatient old solitary believed. They must, after all, have developed into true apostles.

The first part of the *Fiery Arrow* is based on the experience, the contemplative instinct, by which Nicholas himself judged between the things of God and the things of the world. It was a bold declaration that if one lived alone and in silence with God, he received a gift of discernment, a kind of supernatural "taste" with which he could instinctively and spontaneously distinguish the true joys of the divine life from the false, nauseating counterfeit. But if one were unfaithful to solitude and to prayer, he would surely be deluded with false ideas of zeal and, in pretending to seek the salvation of others and the interests of the Church, he would in fact ruin his own soul in the pursuit of unreality.

The second part of the *Sagitta* appeals to the objective standard of the Rule and Nicholas sets about the work of commenting on that document, in order to bring out clearly what are the essential obligations of the Carmelite life.

First of all, he says, there are the three vows common to all religious: poverty, chastity and obedience. But each religious family has a special modality of its own: special means by which its members are to sanctify themselves and consecrate to God the aptitudes which He has given them. Nicholas points to the division between active and contemplative Orders, and here he is at least implicitly in agree-

ment with St. Thomas in admitting the superiority of those
Orders that engage in the apostolic life.[8] It must never be
imagined that the author of the *Fiery Arrow* is concerned
with a partisan defense of the contemplative Orders as such.
Speaking in the practical language of one experienced in
contemplation, he advocates the contemplative life and calls
it superior only for those who have a contemplative vocation: and if it is superior for them this is perhaps because
they do not have the necessary aptitudes for a life of apostolic action.

> God has foreseen that those who would embrace the labors of
> Martha in the cities should be men with aptitude for intellec-
> tual work, for research in Holy Scripture, and men whose
> spiritual life is so firmly established that they can dispense to
> the multitudes the nourishment of the divine word. But the
> simpler sort, those with whom He communes in mystery, these
> the Lord keeps in solitude with the prophet who says: "Lo I
> have gone far off, flying away; and I abode in the wilderness.
> I waited for Him that saved me from pusillanimity of spirit
> and a storm." (Ps. 54:8-9)

Speaking from his own experience on Mount Carmel and
in the west and basing his remarks on the actual persons he
had known in the Order, Nicholas seemed to think that the
Carmelites of his time were not cut out for the apostolic life
except in a very simple and restricted form. But the principles on which he bases this judgment obviously allow for a
totally different viewpoint, once the members of the Order
are adequately prepared for an active mission. However, he
does not envisage any other than the actual situation which
confronted him. He writes only for men whom he knew to
have been called to the hermit life and who had lost their

[8] II IIae Q 188 a 6.c.

way, embracing an active mission for which they were unprepared.

For such men as these, the will of God, manifested by their vocation, was a truly solitary life. Nicholas knows no more satisfactory way of meeting this obligation, that the actual practice he had known and lived on Mount Carmel. The Carmelites, according to him, were obliged by their very vocation to live in isolated cells, in a deserted or rural area.

The Holy Spirit, knowing what is best for each of us, could hardly have inspired without good reason the Rule which says each one of us should have a separate cell. This does not mean neighboring cells, but cells separated from one another, in order that the heavenly spouse and His bride, the contemplative soul, might converse together in the peace of an intimate colloquy . . . Consequently, if we wish to live according to our profession, we must have separated cells, and stay in them, or at least near them, meditating day and night on the Law of the Lord, praying and watching, unless we have other legitimate occupations . . . But you, city dwellers, you have turned the separate cells into a house where you live in common: how can you prepare yourselves for those holy occupations which should be yours? At what hours do you meditate on the Law of the Lord in reflection and prayer? Are not your nights troubled by the remembrance of your vanity, since you pass your day in gossiping, running around, listening, speaking and acting? Your memory is filled with forbidden and impure thoughts to such an extent that your mind is incapable of meditating on anything else . . . If anyone who has made profession of our life finds himself out of his cell, he must ask himself in conscience if he is justified by a legitimate occupation; if he has no reasonable motive, he must get back to his cell. If he disobeys his conscience and does not return to it, he must realize that he is violating his promises. (177, 178)

In reading these bitter reproaches, we can understand why
Nicholas has been considered an extremist by his own Order. It is difficult, if not impossible, to interpret such a text
correctly unless one is able to see through the eyes of the
writer himself. All that is said here is to be understood exclusively from the point of view of one who in actual, concrete fact, was called by God to be a hermit and was fully
aware of it. For such a one, life in the cities would be an
obvious prevarication. But those who came after, who had
made a successful adaptation to the mendicant life, knew
well enough that they could carry on their active, preaching
mission without necessarily being in a state of habitual sin.
On the contrary, though that life had its dangers, it also had
its graces and compensations, and they were no doubt sincerely convinced that the *Fiery Arrow* could no longer be
applied to their case. But then, this could only be because
they had ceased to be what Nicholas believed they ought to
have been, and had become mendicants pure and simple.
Nicholas is not writing for mendicants, but for hermits.
Hence, he insists that for solitaries, life in towns is an infidelity to the Holy Spirit.

Among the reasons for this, he cites first of all ascetic
ones: exterior and interior silence, purity of heart and body,
recollection. But these are not simply ends in themselves.
The positive joys of solitary contemplation are for Nicholas
the most important reason why the hermit should remain in
solitude. These joys are inaccessible in the noise and tur-
moil of the active life. There is probably no more beautiful
chapter in the whole work than that in which he depicts the
hermit's life of praise in union with all creation:

> The beauty of the elements and of the firmament of stars and
> planets harmoniously ordered, attracts us and leads us on to

higher wonders. The birds, in some way putting on the nature of angels, gladden us by intoning their sweet songs. The mountains, according to the prophecy of Isaias, surround us with great sweetness and the hills flow with that milk and honey which are never tasted by those who, in their madness, have chosen the world. These mountains, our conventual brethren who surround us, unite themselves with the psalms which we sing to the glory of the Creator as a lute accompanying words. While we praise the Lord, the roots grow, the grass becomes green, the branches and trees rejoice in their own fashion and applaud our praises. Wonderful flowers, delicately scented, gladden our solitude with their laughter. The silent light of the stars tells us the hours set apart for God's service. Wild growing things cover us with shade and offer us their pleasant fruits. All our sisters the creatures who, in solitude, charm our eyes or our ears, give us rest and comfort. In silence they give forth their beauty like a song, encouraging our soul to praise the wonderful Creator. Isaias speaks to us in figure of this joy of solitude and of the desert: "The land that was desolate and impassable shall be glad and the wilderness shall rejoice, and shall flourish like the lily. It shall bud forth and blossom and rejoice in prayer and praise." (Isa. 35:1-2) So also in the Psalm: "The beautiful places of the wilderness shall grow fat: and the hills shall be girded about with joy." (Ps. 64:13) (182, 183)

There is no need to crown this beautiful passage with an obvious platitude by calling it Franciscan, as if St. Francis had a monoply on the contemplation of the Creator in His creation. This view of creation is so traditionally and essentially Christian that it is found in all the saints who have been at all articulate on the subject, and perhaps not least surprisingly in some of the most austere. It is certainly found in St. John of the Cross—in fact all through the *Fiery Arrow* we hear echoes of the saint of the *Dark Night* who is also the contemplative of the *Spiritual Canticle* and of the *Living Flame*. The principles are the same, the conclusions are identical. In order to seek true joy, the joy of God in all things, renounce joy in all things. That is, do not trouble and distract your soul with a concern that yearns for this or that limited joy, seeking happiness now here and now there, restlessly passing from one to the other, Renounce the vain quest, give your whole heart of God, and He Himself in return will give you joy in all things.

> In order to arrive at having pleasure in everything, desire to have pleasure in nothing . . .

> Through the eye that is purged from the joys of sight, there comes to the soul a spiritual joy, directed to God in all things that are seen, whether Divine or profane. Through the ear that is purged from the joy of hearing, there comes to the soul joy most spiritual an hundredfold directed to God in all that it hears, be it Divine or profane. Even so is it with the other senses when they are purged. For even as in the state of innocence all that our first parents saw and heard and ate in Paradise furnished them with greater sweetness of contemplation, so that the sensual part of their nature might be duly subjected to, and ordered by, reason; even so the man whose sense is purged from all things of sense and made subject to the spirit, receives, in his very first motion, the delight of delectable knowledge and contemplation of God.[9]

We can sum up our discussion of the *Fiery Arrow* with the following conclusions. It has certain superficial resemblances to the anti-mendicant tracts of the 13th century, but in reality it is an entirely different kind of thing. To reject it along with William of Saint Amour would be to misun-

[9] Ascent of Mount Carmel: i, xiii, vol. 1 p. 63 and iii, xxvi, id. p. 288.

derstand completely its deep and undying message. It is not an attack on the apostolic life, or on the mendicant Orders. Far rather it is a defense of an original, unique and quite unusual combination of contemplation and apostolate. It is a defense of a religious family that would necessarily always be isolated and small, and of an apostolate that would never be fruitful on a large external scale. The insistence of Nicholas on the Rule of St. Albert is less juridical than the spiritual, and he is not concerned with defending contemplation or action as specific ends and works to be achieved. On the contrary, what he insists on is the concrete, we might say existential value of the life itself that he had known on Mount Carmel. What he feared—and not without reason,—was that this unique life would be altogether lost to the Church and would vanish from the world.

That the Carmelites might go through a kind of "dialectical" development and reach a new solution, beyond and above the apparent opposition that troubled Nicholas the Frenchman, seems not to have occurred to the author of the *Fiery Arrow*. But in any case, for the dialectic to be valid, the new solution would have to include within itself all the values inherent in both the thesis and the antithesis that had been transcended. The Carmelites would have to be in the truest sense both hermits, and apostles. They would have to be something more than simple solitaries, more than ordinary preachers. They would have to be men of God who were "prophets" living and acting, by their poverty and nakedness of spirit, according to the austere laws of the desert, directly and continually dependent on God the Holy Spirit.

IV . *Reform and apostolate*

The whole subsequent history of Carmel is in fact the history of this endeavor. Whether the solution was ever fully achieved in the Middle Ages can perhaps be a matter for dispute. At any rate, the Order survived, prospered, declined, revived in many ways and in many places. There was the 15th century reform of Bl. John Soreth which brought into existence those Carmelite nuns who were to be reformed again by St. Theresa of Avila. In 1567, Father John Baptist Rubeo, General of the Carmelites, coming to apply in Spain the decrees of the Council of Trent for the reform of religious, laid down this principle as the basis for the renewal of life in what had now been for three hundred years a mendicant and apostolic Order:

> The chief and primitive ideal of the inhabitants of Mount Carmel—an ideal which every Carmelite must imitate and pursue—is this: day and night they must consecrate all the efforts of which they are capable to uniting their soul and their spirit to God the Father by meditation, contemplation and uninterrupted love. And this is to be done not only in a habitual fashion but also actually.[10]

St. Theresa herself had no other purpose in her reform than a return to the solitude and contemplation of the primitive Carmelite ideal. She says so explicitly:

> All of us who wear this sacred habit of Carmel are called to prayer and contemplation because that was the first principle

[10] Quoted by Bruno de Jesus-Marie, in "Traversées Historiques," *Etudes Carmelitaines*, Avril 1935, p. 18.

of our Order and because we are descended from the line of those holy Fathers of ours from Mount Carmel who sought this treasure, this precious pearl of which we speak, in such great solitude and with such contempt for the world.[11]

Yet at the same time, the reformer of Carmel clearly conceived that the prayers of the Discalced Nuns had an apostolic object: they were to pray especially for the salvation of souls and for the work of the priests engaged in the work of the Counter-Reformation. Such apostolic prayer was, indeed, "the principal reason for which the Lord has brought us together in this house." [12]

Hence, in one word, it is clear that the Discalced Carmelite Reform was a return to the primitive spirit of solitude, but at the same time a renewal of the apostolic spirit. But it can be said that this renewal was, in fact, given an original character of its own by the circumstances of the time.

It would be tedious and out of place here to enter into all the intricacies of the history of the Discalced Carmelite Reform in this matter. Let it be sufficient to indicate that once the reform broke off from the "Calced" and became autonomous in Spain, it was divided from within into two strongly opposed factions, especially after the death of St. Theresa who "protected Fr. Jerome Gratian against Doria and against himself." [13] On the one hand there was Fr. Doria, the hermit of Pastrana, the ferocious partisan of strict observance, solitude and austerity before all else. The sagacity of St. Theresa had held him in check as long as she was alive. As soon as she was dead, Doria would make short work of Fr. Jerome Gratian whom he considered a "radical," and who seemed to be undermining the reform with his zeal for

---

[11] Interior Castle, v, i. Vol. ii (Peers trans.) p. 247.
[12] Way of Perfection, iii, vol. ii, p. 10.
[13] cf. Fr. Bruno de Jesus Marie, art, cit. p. 25.

apostolic work and even for foreign missions. Once again it
was the old opposition that had excited such anguish in the
writer of the *Fiery Arrow*. In between the two stood St. John
of the Cross, who transcended them both, who included in
himself all that was good in either of them: who was an
austere lover of solitude, but more prudent than Doria because he knew that solitude itself could become a fetish, an
object of immoderate attachment. He knew that the love of
austerity could become a mere "penance of beasts." He fully
understood and carried out St. Theresa's apostolic ideals
without being swept away by the volatile enthusiasms of a
Gratian. He it was who embodied in himself the true prophetic spirit of Carmel, and it is remarkable that of the
three, he was the one who was externally the least fiery,
the least impressive, the most obscure. Of the three he was
the most silent, the most retiring, the truest solitary, the greatest contemplative. But also, at the same time, he was of the
three the greatest apostle, the one who had the surest and
deepest effect on other people. These were not souls whom
he had hunted out with the busy zeal of an aggressive con-
vert maker: they were people who had been brought to him
by God, without his knowing how they came to him. And
they were transformed, as a result, without either he or they
knowing what had happened.

The most remarkable thing about St. John of the Cross
and Saint Theresa of Avila is that in their lives as well as in
their words they represent the perfect flowering of the
Carmelite ideal as it was conceived by Nicholas the Frenchman and glorified in the *Fiery Arrow*. The mystical works of
St. John of the Cross are simply the flowering of seeds that
germinate on every page of the 13th century encyclical of
the hermit of Carmel. The "desert" doctrine of the Carmelite mystics is again the realization of all that is implied in

the aspirations of Nicholas the Frenchman. Yet it cannot be said that the life of the first Discalced Carmelites was in every physical detail the life demanded by the earliest version of the Rule of St. Albert and defended with such ardor by Nicholas in the *Fiery Arrow*. It might at first sight seem that Doria and his party were tending, by their austerity and violent defense of primitive eremitism, toward a greater conformity with the ideals of Nicholas. But this is not the case. It is in Theresa and John of the Cross that we find the true successors to the one who fired that original arrow. Whether or not they were acquainted with the document is not, of itself, particularly important.

But it must be admitted that the apostolic ideal of a St. Theresa was much more far reaching than that of Nicholas the Frenchman. True, but her situation was different. The Carmelites had for centuries been established as a mendicant Order and they had a definite function to fulfil in the Church. They could fulfil that function and still return closer to the primitive ideal. This could be done in two ways: by a recovery of the original spirit of solitude and prayer, and by a reduction of the apostolate to a more occasional and more specialized level. And so, though the Duscalced Carmelites did not reproduce in every detail the life of the first hermits on the Holy Mountain, they did revive the primitive spirit of the Order in a very authentic form particularly adapted to the post-Tridentine counter-reformation.

In spite of the apparent "victory" that rewarded the centralizing politics of Doria and his party, in spite of the fact that Gratian was broken and John of the Cross died, the policies of Doria did not prevail. On the contrary, it was the apostolic and missionary ideal, which had been the ideal of Theresa of Avila, came out on top in the end. Indeed,

Carmelite Friars began to cross the seas to Africa and Asia, and Mount Carmel itself was to be reconquered and re-settled by them.

In 1582, even before the death of St. Theresa, Gratian had sent a party of Carmelites to make a foundation in Ethiopia which was almost as bad as sending them to the moon. When the party was shipwrecked and drowned, the Doria faction hailed the event with ferocious satisfaction as a mani-fest sign of divine displeasure with the apostolic party. A first party of friars that was sent out to the Congo was cap-tured by British pirates and marooned. Renewed satisfac-tion on the part of the hermits! A second group which suc-ceeded in getting to the Congo was left to die there by Doria who abandoned them after he got in power. Never-theless the missionary ideal persisted. Eliseus of the Martyrs, who was to be provincial of the Carmelites in Mexico, well knew the apostolic zeal of St. John of the Cross, who believed that "it was not the will of God that the Order of His Mother should be limited and restricted to the boundaries of Spain, but that it should extend and spread out to every part of the Church provided that the institution of the Order could be kept there." [14]

These last words are very important, and whatever may have been St. John's sense of the apostolate, he, of all the Carmelite saints, certainly came closest to the author of the *Fiery Arrow* in his sense of the primacy of contemplation. We need only to quote here the celebrated passage from the *Spiritual Canticle* in which he says that the Carmelite who has been drawn into union with God by prayer should not be disturbed with active works, unless of course God Himself commands and inspires them. This is the obvious

[14] Quoted in art. cit. p. 26.

development of the doctrine expressed in the *Fiery Arrow*. It is worth remembering.

> When it reaches that estate (of unitive love) it befits it not to be occupied in other outward acts and exercises which might keep it back, however little, from that abiding in love with God, although they may greatly conduce to the service of God; for a very little of this pure love is more precious in the sight of God and the soul, and of greater profit to the Church, even though the soul appear to be doing nothing, than are all the works together. . . . Therefore if the soul have aught of this degree of solitary love, great wrong would be done to it and to the Church if, even but for a brief space, one should endeavor to busy it in active or outward affairs, of however great moment . . . Let those then that are great actives, that think to girdle the world with their outward works and their preachings, take not that here they would bring far more profit to the Church and be far more pleasing to God (apart from the good example which they would give of themselves) if they spent even half this time in abiding with God in prayer, even had they not reached such a height as this.[15]

This is a weighty statement, and one which disturbs us in our anxiety to be always producing some visible result to justify our existence in the Church. Clearly it cannot be adduced as an excuse to evade the normal duties of religious life. But it certainly shows that St. John of the Cross, for all his apostolic zeal, would never have countenanced the foundation of a Carmelite community under circumstances that would involve the Friars in extremely burdensome and continual active works, to the detriment of their main object which is solitude and contemplation. This did not prevent

[15] *Spiritual Canticle*, xxix, 2. Vol. ii (Peers trans.) p. 346.

him from desiring missionary foundations in Africa or America. When Doria was engineering his disgrace, St. John thought of retiring to the Carmelite foundation in Mexico, but died before this could be achieved. And Theresa of Jesus had wept at the convent grille when she heard, from a Franciscan missionary, of the millions of souls being lost in the Americas. Though the Doria party firmly refused to spread the Theresian reform outside of Spain, the gordian knot was cut by Pope Clement VIII who established the Discalced in Italy in a separate province, and instructed them to make foundations "at Rome and in all parts of the world." [16]

Carmelites established themselves in Persia (1607), Mesopotamia, Syria, India, Central and South America, Africa, the East Indies, and in 1631 a Spaniard of the Province of Genoa, Prosper of the Holy Spirit, returned to live as a hermit in a cave on Mount Carmel. The Friars had come back to the Holy Mountain of Elias and of the Blessed Virgin! This symbolic gesture was conceived in one of the desert hermitages of the Discalced Friars, and this important movement deserves consideration in the concluding words of our study.

v . *Carmelite deserts*

It has been said that the institution of the "deserts" was the closest approach to the primitive Carmelite ideal made by any reform of the Order since the middle ages. The author of the idea was Thomas of Jesus, and it is significant that he was first of all a faithful follower of St. Theresa and of St. John of the Cross, and secondly that he was of the apostolic group, rather than of the Doria party. When Thomas of Jesus first proposed to Doria the foundation of a "desert"

[16] Fr. Bruno de Jesus Marie, art. cit. p. 27.

—that is to say of a remote and isolated community where a small number would live as true hermits in separate cells, Doria refused permission on the ground that it would disrupt the Order and draw "all the best men" away from the cities into solitude. This paradoxical admission shows us at once how complex was the character of the organizer and hermit who took command of the Discalced Carmelites after the death of St. Theresa! Thomas of Jesus obediently renounced his plan. But it happened that one day in 1591, when he was professor and vice rector in the Carmelite house of studies at Alcala, he was re-reading his notes on the plan for a desert foundation and, being called suddenly away, left them lying open on his table. The rector chanced to see them, and becoming enthusiastic about the project, brought up the subject of its possibilities. Interest was aroused. The plan was once again presented discretely to Doria who, this time, accepted it. The definitory decreed the establishment of a desert foundation. A benefactor offered land, and the first Carmelite desert of Bolarque, in an isolated rocky valley of Castille, came into existence. Four Friars hastened to the spot and the first small buildings were erected in the summer of 1592.

What was the nature and purpose of a Carmelite "desert"? Physically it resembled a Camaldolese *eremo:* a village of separate cells, with a chapel, a gatehouse, an enclosure wall. There were also more isolated hermitages in the woods, to which the brethren might retire at certain periods of the year for more complete solitude. The population of a "desert" consisted of some twenty to twenty-four friars and a maximum of six lay brothers. Of the friars, four were permanent hermits, assigned to the desert at their own request for the rest of their days. Of these, one was the Prior, chosen for his contemplative wisdom, love of solitude, and aptitude to direct and moderate the lives of his companions. The majority of the hermits were temporary residents, assigned to the desert (usually at their own request) for periods of several months or for an entire year. In some provinces it was required that men spend a certain time in the desert before ordination to the priesthood or before being sent to a foreign mission.

Generally speaking, the desert was regarded as a special function of that contemplative solitude and necessary in an apostolic Order, though it would not be quite correct to say that the friars went to the desert *to prepare themselves for* apostolic work. That would be a misleading conception. Contemplative solitude has no ulterior purpose, and when it seems to have one, it becomes degenerate, and ceases to be what it pretends to be. The function of the Carmelite desert was not to be merely a place of retirement to which one would have access *before* apostolic labors in order to prepare oneself spiritually or *after* apostolic labor in order to recover and rest. No such pragmatism could ever be fully compatible with the true Carmelite ideal. On the contrary, it would be truer to say that the desert was a place to which the friars went to be most truly what they were called, Carmelites, faithful sons of the Virgin of Carmel and spiritual descendants of Elias. The purpose of the deserts was to give them access to that pure and perfect climate of solitude without which they would never fully be themselves. Even where the deserts do not exist (and in most provinces of the Carmelites they do not exist today), wherever the authentic spirit of Carmel prevails, Friars who have never seen a desert nevertheless have in their heart the hunger for solitude and prayer which only such a place as this could provide.

Even where deserts do not exist, the spirit of solitude and

contemplation is ever present in the Order. It is inescapable because of the fervor and the primitive purity of the Discalced Carmelite nuns, who, like the Carthusians, have had the distinction of never needing another reform.

In the seventeenth century there were deserts everywhere in the Order, even in Mexico. They were particularly numerous in Spain, Italy and France. Many ordinary Carmelite monasteries, though in towns, managed to maintain hermitages in their large gardens. An interesting history of these desert houses, unfortunately incomplete, was written by a historian of the Order, Father Benedict Mary of the Holy Cross.[17] He described twenty-two deserts of the Order of which all but one had ceased to exist in his time. But since then, especially since the second world war, the general return to contemplation which has manifested itself in various other forms, also produced this revival of a Carmelite desert in France. The Order took over an abandoned Camaldolese hermitage at Roquebrune, in the mountains of southern France. This became a desert for the French and Belgian Provinces of the Discalced Carmelite Friars. Two other deserts also exist in Spain and quite naturally there is talk of deserts in other provinces of the Order. There is no reason why such a desert should not soon be founded in the United States, and such a foundation would certainly correspond to the deepest desires of several American Carmelite friars known to the author.

Since this is the case, it is perhaps not useless to bring back to mind the strangely moving pages of the *Fiery Arrow*, and to reflect on the reasons why the document was so long passed over and forgotten.

It is true that the author of the *Fiery Arrow* was in some sense a failure, an idealist who rebelled against the trend of

[16] Les saints deserts des carmes dechaussés, Paris, 1927.

the times without being able to change anything. Let us be careful not to reject his testimony out of a kind of secret, semi-pelagian pragmatism which flourishes more vigorously than we realize among us today. There are signs that a revival of solitary life in its various forms is of great importance for the Church today. One of these forms is the Carmelite Desert, and here no special complications stand in the way of the project being easily realized. The Carmelites themselves have an easy and obvious way of putting to practical use such suggestions of their primitive tradition as can be applied to the needs of our day.

What about the rest of us? Have we something more than this to learn from the primitive tradition of Carmel? I think so. It may very well be that Nicholas the Frenchman was very far ahead of his time. It certainly seems that the very original form of contemplative life which he tried vainly to preserve in its simplicity in the 13th century, is one of the things we need, and ought to seek to establish in our own day. I refer to the conception of a small eremitical community practicing solitude, prayer, manual labor and the traditional exercises of the solitary life, but at the same time permitting and envisaging an informal apostolate, consisting of restricted, somewhat "special" contacts with people outside. This, after all, was something like the life planned by Charles de Foucauld for his hermits in the Sahara. His dream was never realized in his lifetime. It has been realized, in a modified form, by the Little Brothers of Jesus. But the Little Brothers, like the Carmelites of St. Simon Stock, are mostly in cities and towns. Their vocation is to work among men. There still remains a need for a purely eremitical community, isolated and quiet, to which perhaps a few people might have access by invitation or otherwise. The outside contacts would have to be small and selective.

There would be no question of a habitual apostolate. But there would be room for a contemplative and spiritual dialogue with laypeople or members of other Orders. The fruit would be the extension of the spiritual and intellectual lives: of contemplation in a broad and healthy sense, integrated in every form of human existence. Ideally speaking, such a community could engage in a very fruitful dialogue with non-Catholic intellectuals, with Oriental thinkers, with artists and philosophers, scientists and politicians—but on a very simple, radical and primitive level, though in full cognizance of the problems of our time. This is just one example that occurs, of a possible application to our day of the primitive ideal of a solitary, contemplative and apostolic group, with a primitive and "prophetic" character—a voice crying in the wilderness to prepare the ways of the Lord.

CHRISTIANITY AND TOTALITARIANISM

The task of the Christian in our time is the same as it has always been: to build the Kingdom of God in this world. To manifest Christ in individuals and in society—or rather to allow the Savior to manifest His hidden presence in the world by the charity and unity, in one Body, of those He came to save. "That they all may be one as Thou Father in me and I in Thee, that they also may be one in us: that the world may believe that Thou hast sent me." This task is of course ultimately spiritual and eschatalogical, for the earthly manifestation of the Kingdom of God is still only a shadow of the eternal Kingdom that is to come. However, the spiritual character of the Kingdom cannot be made into a pretext for ignoring the temporal happiness and welfare of man in this present life. This may have been a temptation in the past. Those who yielded to it may perhaps have been excusable in their day. But it is no longer permitted to us to close our eyes to the danger of so grave an error. We must plainly and courageously face the fact that "building the Kingdom of God in this world" in preparation for the ultimate and eschatalogical revelation of the Kingdom in eternity means in fact *building a better world here and now:—* a better world for man to live in, and thus save his immortal soul.

Why is this so? Because man is not a pure spirit: his life in the world is a bodily life. He needs food, shelter, protection, comradeship and work. He lives as a member of a visible society. His interior and spiritual life, in a word, his salvation, depends in large measure on his ability to provide a normal and reasonable standard of living for himself and his family, to take part freely in the political, artistic and intellectual life of the world, and above all to serve and love his God.

The Kingdom of God is the Kingdom of Love: but where freedom, justice, education, and a decent standard of living are not to be had in society, how can the Kingdom of Love be built in that society? A starving man has little capacity to think about love. It is true, great saints can live and thrive in conditions that would be impossible for the average man. But the Kingdom of God is not made up exclusively of great saints: it is a living, Mystical organism made up of *average* men, with their weaknesses, their limitations, their good will, their talents, their deficiencies—all taken up and divinized by the Holy Spirit, so that Christ lives and manifests Himself in one and all. We who have been called, as average men, to live in this great mystery of the One Christ, must take care to see that we build for one another a world of justice, decent living, honest labor, peace and truth, fully recognizing that without these conditions we can only with great difficulty protect our weakness against sin, loss of faith, and ultimate despair.

Christians are not the only ones in the world who are
faced with this need to build a new and better society. Indeed, it must be said to our confusion that we have not
even been the first to undertake this most pressing task of
our century. Others, whose good will we cannot doubt,
have rushed ahead and taken upon themselves the responsibility which we ourselves had been perhaps slow to assume.
Yet their good will cannot permit us to ignore the terrible
blunders which they have committed in their attempts to
build a better world without love, without Christ, and without God.

It is true that Love and Religion tend to lose their meaning and become mere words in a world where Justice, Peace,
and Humanity have been so often and so cynically be-
trayed. But it is even more true that a society that attempts
to create Justice, Peace and Humane living without God,
ends without fail by falling headlong into an even greater
injustice, an even more terrible addiction to war, cruelty
and violence.

Those who seek to build a better world without God are
those who, trusting in money, power, technology and organization, deride the spiritual strength of faith and love
and fix all their hopes on a huge monolithic society, having
a monopoly over all power, all production, and even over
the minds of its members. But to alienate the spirit of man
by subjecting him to such monstrous indignity is to make
injustice and violence inevitable. By such means we may
indeed increase economic production but in doing so we
will only make the world worse.

The fact that the Church is the Mystical Body of Christ
immediately sets it apart from every form of "aggregation,"
or "collectivity." If the Church were merely a moral body, a

social organization, there would be no spiritual mystery about the union of her many members into one body. They would simply be united by common interests and a common purpose. But the Church is something far greater and more mysterious than this. The unity of the members of Christ is such that together they form one Person, One Christ, and yet each one personally "is Christ."

Christ the Lord is all in all, and present in each one of His members. Christ is not Head of the Church in the same way that a Dictator is Head of a Totalitarian State. By his authority and power, the Dictator imposes his policies on every individual in the state, controlling them in and through a vast political organization. Christ rules His faithful first of all from within, with the power and authority of supernatural life and of grace. It is because of the inner movement of the Holy Spirit the "believers" unite themselves freely with one another in the Church, under the authority of a visible head who represents Christ on earth. The Church as a visible society has, of course, her organization, laws and discipline. But these are all secondary, and relatively unimportant compared with the principle of inner and spiritual unity which is the charity of Christ. Charity can only be exercised among free individual men. Charity is the mark of a *person*, not of an organization.

The Church therefore is not an army or a mass-movement in which the individual loses himself. When the prophets preached the Messianic Kingdom of Peace, they based their preaching on justice and mercy which implied a profound respect for the rights and integrity of the human person. And when Christ, in the New Testament, preached the Kingdom of God, He opened the way only to individuals. No one can enter the Kingdom except by his own personal decision.

We are not saved *en masse*. Masses indeed may be called, but only individuals are chosen because only individuals can respond to a call by a free choice of their own. The Church is not, and has never been merely for the mass-man, the passive, inert man who drifts with the crowd and never decides anything for himself.

The mass-man is material for a mass-movement because he is easily transformed into a fanatic. That is why the mass-movement is so congenial to fanatics, and seeks to keep the fanaticism of its members at a high pitch. Indeed, when the members of a mass-movement begin to lose their fanatical hatred of everything that is *not* the movement, then that movement itself begins to die. This is a truth which Hitler openly admitted, and it explains the frantic insistence of the Russians on maintaining an iron curtain and preaching virulent hatred of the unknown world that lies beyond it.

In spite of this, there are as we know many Russians who instinctively realize that outside the Iron Curtain are millions of persons who, like themselves, love peace and do not want war. This instinct of love, and identification of oneself with the foreigner and stranger, this ability to find oneself in another, which alone can preserve world peace, is a fundamentally Christian instinct. Its continued presence in the Western World is due to the influence of our Christian past. Woe to us if this heritage is ever lost!

Nothing is so harmful to the Church as fanaticism. And it is harmful precisely because it produces an *ersatz* of Christian fervor and unity. The fanaticism of a mass-movement has the semblance of a unanimous spiritual front—the dedication of members to a common purpose to resist error and stamp out evil. It is precisely this semblance of spirituality and dedication that makes fanaticism deadly.

Fanaticism is never really spiritual because it is not *free*. It is not free because it is not enlightened. It cannot judge between good and evil, truth and falsity, because it is blinded by prejudice. Faith and prejudice have a common need to rely on authority and in this they can sometimes be confused by one who does not understand their true nature. But faith rests on the authority of love while prejudice rests on the pseudo-authority of hatred. Everyone who has read the Gospel realizes that in order to be a Christian one must give up being a fanatic, because Christianity is love. Love and fanaticism are incompatible. Fanaticism thrives on aggression. It is destructive, revengeful and sterile. Fanaticism is all the more virulent in proportion as it springs from *inability* to love, from incapacity to reciprocate human understanding.

Fanaticism refuses to look at another man as a person. It regards him only as a thing. He is either a "member" or he is not a member. He is either part of one's own mob, or he is outside the mob. Woe to him, above all, if he stands outside the mob with the mute protest of his individual personality! That was what happened at the Crucifixion of Christ. Christ, the Incarnate Son of God, came as a Person, seeking the understanding, the acceptance and the love of free persons. He found Himself face to face with a compact fanatical group, that wanted nothing of His Person. They feared His disturbing uniqueness. It was necessary, as Caiphas said, that this "one man should die for the nation"— that the individual Person, and above all *this* Person, should be sacrificed to the collectivity. From its very birth, Christianity has been categorically opposed to everything that savors of the mass-movement.

A mass-movement always places the "cause" above the individual person, and sacrifices the person to the interests of the movement. Thus it empties the person of all that is his own, takes him out of himself, casts him in a mold which endows him with the ideas and aspirations of the group rather than his own. There is nothing wrong in the person sacrificing himself for society: there can be times when this is right and necessary, and in the sacrifice the person will find himself on a higher level. But in the case of a mass-movement the emptying of the individual turns him into a husk, a mask, a puppet which is used and manipulated at will by the leaders of the movement. The individual ceases to be a person and becomes simply a "member," a "thing" which serves a cause, not by thinking and willing, but by being pushed about like a billiard ball, in accordance with the interests of the cause.

Contrast this with the teaching of Christ, for whom the soul of the individual was more important than the most sacred laws and rites, since these exist only for the sake of persons, and not vice versa. "The sabbath was made for man and not man for the sabbath." (Mark 2:27) Christ even placed the bodily health and well being of individuals before the law of the sabbath. One of the bitterest complaints made against Him was that He cured on the sabbath.

A mass-movement readily exploits the discontent and frustration of large segments of the population which for some reason or other cannot face the responsibility of being persons and standing on their own feet. But give these persons a movement to join, a cause to defend, and they will go to any extreme, stop at no crime, intoxicated as they are by the slogans that give them a pseudo-religious sense of transcending their own limitations. The member of the mass-movement, afraid of his own isolation and his own weakness as an individual, cannot face the task of discovering within himself the spiritual power and integrity which can be called forth only by love. Instead of this, he seeks a movement that will protect his weakness with a wall of anonymity and justify his acts by the sanction of collective glory and power. All the better if this is done out of hatred, for hatred is always easier and less subtle than love. It does not have to respect reality, as love does. It does not have to take account of individual cases. Its solutions are simple and easy. It makes its decisions by a simple glance at a face, a colored skin, a uniform. It identifies the enemy by an accent, an unfamiliar turn of speech, an appeal to concepts that are difficult to understand. And then fanaticism knows what to do. Here is something unfamiliar. This is not "ours." This must be brought into line—or destroyed.

Here is the great temptation of the modern age, this universal infection of fanaticism, this plague of intolerance, prejudice and hate which flows from the crippled nature of man who is afraid of love and does not dare to be a person. It is against this temptation most of all that the Christian must labor with inexhaustible patience and love, in silence, perhaps in repeated failure, seeking tirelessly to restore, wherever he can, and first of all in himself, the capacity of love and understanding which makes man the living image of God.

In the Old Testament, the Chosen People followed Moses as a group toward the Promised Land. As a community they entered with Josue into the Kingdom of Promise. It was sufficient to be part of the community that kept God's law, and the rest was taken care of. But in the New Testament, the message of salvation is addressed not to a group or a totality but to individuals. *Si quis vult* . . . "If any man, any person, decides and wills to follow me . . ." In the New Testament salvation is a matter of a free per-

sonal decision to accept and to follow Christ, to do the will
of Christ, to please Him, to be His friend. The ritual of
baptism is sufficient evidence of the care the Church takes
to treat her children as individual persons, and to show a
supreme respect for their freedom. Only a person can say
"volo" "I will." The Christian is not saved as a member of a
mob, by joining in mass acclamations and allowing himself
to be lost and submerged in the vast anonymous exultation
of a totality. The *Alleluia* of the victorious Church of Christ
is indeed the acclamation of a "great multitude which no
man can number" (Apoc. 7:9) but it is made up of the
"*Volo*," the declaration of each one that he is a member of
Christ, a friend of Christ. And this witness may often be
sealed by the Christian's own blood in martyrdom. Religious
vows are not merely the individual's consecration of himself
to the service of a good cause, not merely a matter of im-
mersing oneself in the anonymity of an Order—religious profession is the act by which one declares that he is before all
else a friend, even a spouse, of Christ. It is not a renunciation
of personality, but like martyrdom, its highest affirmation.

The members of a mass-movement may perhaps choose
to become units in the totalitarian community: more often
they are dragged into it or they drift into it passively, without too definite a decision. In any case, membership in a
mass-movement is too often merely an "escape from freedom," a renunciation of personal responsibility, in order to
live not by one's own mind and one's own freedom but by
the thought and decisions of the group: the party line, the
will of the leader. The disastrous consequences of this renunciation of moral responsibility on the part of the individual has been made clear by the unbelievable atrocities
committed in police states all over the world in the last
thirty years. These things have been done "with a good

conscience" by people who have ceased to think and decide for themselves, carried away by the hypnotic effect of feeling themselves lost in a huge entity vastly more powerful and more effective in its actions than an individual could ever be. The member of the mass-movement loses his sense of limitation, weakness, fallibility, in the unlimited power and infallibility of the group.

When Christ called the "poor in spirit" blessed, He did not preach the abdication of our human dignity, He did not preach flight from individual responsibility and from the risks and limitations it implies. On the contrary, who is more poor in spirit than the man who takes the risk of standing on his own feet, who tries to realize his own fallibility and struggles to decide in his own conscience what is the will of God? From the moment that we break away from the reassuring passivity and confusion which surrounds us on all sides as we drift with the stream of the world, we become aware of our own insecurity, our fallibility, and we "work out our salvation in fear and trembling."

Take the moral teaching of St. Paul to the Ephesians or Corinthians, as an example. The life of the pagan world, with its idolatry, its comfortable, accepted rituals and superstitions, its drunkenness, its luxury and its self-indulgence, created an atmosphere of warm, delusive irresponsibility in which the individual could drift along without worrying too much. This is not hard for us to visualize since our present day society is just about the same. We too feel the risk and insecurity that comes when we nerve ourselves to break away from this passivity, to resist those who try to "deceive us with vain words" (Ephesians 5:6) to "be not partakers with them" (id. 7) and "to be no more children tossed to and fro with every wind of doctrine by the wickedness of men . . . who walk in the vanity of their mind, having their understanding darkened, being alienated from the life of God . . . who despairing have given themselves up to lasciviousness . . . and covetousness" (Ephesians 4:14-19).

It is the man who identifies himself with a powerful group, glories in its display of might and fills his mouth and his head with its jargon, who ceases to be poor in spirit because he no longer has to take the responsibility of thinking and willing as a fallible person.

Personality means at once glory and lowliness, power and risk. When he is called upon to answer for his actions, the person who stands alone is weak and helpless indeed if he finds himself faced with a group that does not approve of his action. And yet he is in possession of great spiritual power if his personal decision has been made in the light of truth, with the testimony of a good conscience, as the act of a child of God. "What then shall we say to these things? If God be for us, who is against us? . . . Who shall accuse against the elect of God? God that justifieth." (Romans 8:31-33)

The individual Christian does not stand absolutely alone. He who has in his heart the testimony of Christ and of the Holy Spirit, who stands firm in the love of God and of his truth, who clings to the truth not because of a temporal power and glory that are seen, but because of the invisible glory of God in the inmost depths of his being, in faith— such a one is united with all who share the same hope, the same faith, the same love. He is one with those who are filled with the same Spirit. His unity with them is expressed by an exterior confession of faith, by fidelity to the same laws, by participation in the same liturgical worship of the All Holy One. He is a member of the visible Church, the

Mystical Body of Christ. But these things alone do not constitute the essence of his unity with his brethren and with Christ, which is interior and spiritual. Of the Christian's interior union with Christ and his brethren, his faith and obedience and worship are only the outward sign not the whole spiritual essence.

Hence there must be something more in the Christian life and apostolate, than merely persuading Christians to adhere to the same doctrinal propositions, to obey the same laws, and frequent the same sacraments. If we are content with merely exterior practice of our religion we will tend to make Christianity another of the mass-movements that cover the face of the earth. Then the Christian, rather than a free man, humbled by the consciousness of his responsibility, tends to become another fanatic who allows himself the worst excesses and excuses them easily on the ground that he is "defending the faith" or "fighting for the Church." A timely example: the readiness some Christians might have today to accept the idea of an all-out atomic surprise attack on Russia, and their approval of the most drastic and cruel methods in order to "stamp out communism." Such things are complacently "justified" by the argument that the communists are atheists, enemies of God, and hence "outside the law." The example may seem a gratuitous supposition. Let us hope there are few such Christians in the world, or none at all. Yet we cannot forget the frightful barbarities perpetrated by the Western Crusaders in Constantinople, desecrating Greek Churches, sacking monasteries and committing all sorts of other crimes, confident that these were acts proper to a holy war! Such incomprehension of the law and love of Christ seems almost unbelievable. Yet the study of history shows us these things and others like them repeated over and over again. By such ac-

tions the Kingdom of God is not built, it is destroyed: or
would be if the gates of hell could prevail against it.

The union that binds the members of Christ together
is not the union of proud confidence in the power of an
organization. The Church is united by the *humility* as well
as by the charity of her members. Hers is the union that
comes from the consciousness of individual fallibility and
poverty, from the humility which recognizes its own limitations and accepts them, the meekness that cannot take upon
itself to condemn, but can only forgive because it is conscious that it has itself been forgiven by Christ. The union
of Christians is a union of friendship and mercy, a bearing
of one anothers' burdens in the sharing of divine forgiveness. Christian forgiveness is not confined merely to those
who are members of the Church. To be a Christian one
must love all men, including not only one's own enemies
but even those who claim to be the "enemies of God."
"Whosoever is angry with his brother shall be in danger of
the judgment . . . Love your enemies, do good to them
that hate you, pray for them that persecute and calumniate
you, that you may be the children of your Father who is in
heaven." (Matt. 5:22, 44, 45). The solidarity of the Christian community is not based on the awareness that the
Church has authority to cast out and to anathematize, but
on the realization that Christ has given her the power to
forgive sin in His Name and to welcome the sinner to the
banquet of His love in the Holy Eucharist. More than this,
the Church is aware of her divine mission to bring forgiveness and peace *to all men*. This means not only that the
sacraments are there for all who will approach them, but
that Christians themselves must bring love, mercy and justice into the lives of their neighbors, in order to reveal to

them the presence of Christ in His Church. This can only be done if all Christians strive generously to love and serve all men with whom they come into contact in their daily lives.

It has been repeatedly pointed out that the Mystical Body of Christ is not an organization but an organism. However, if this is to be an intuition that has meaning, and not just a verbal formula, we must realize that an organism is a living thing, and that it is ruled by the laws of life. Life is subject to its own laws. It does not allow itself to be governed by anything outside itself. The life which Christ came to give to the world is His own life, His love, and His freedom. He Himself is the "way, the truth and the life" both of the Christian and of the Church. Our task as Christians is to continue on earth that same life which Christ lived among us. Each individual Christian embarks upon a life in which he will govern his conduct by the pattern of the Gospels, and on the Christ-likeness of the saints. But in order to understand both the Gospels and the example of the saints, he must be not only guided exteriorly by the Church but also interiorly formed and taught by the Holy Spirit. Such a life cannot be reduced to mere external conformity to the patterns and norms of a given social group, no matter how Christian may be its intentions. Each Christian must work out his own salvation, as a member of Christ, and work it out in union with others. But the new circumstances of each age in the life of the Church confronts each new generation of Christians with problems and solutions for which the past offers no fully satisfactory example.

This means that each Christian has a truly creative mission in the society of his time. He has to begin anew, under new conditions, the great task of helping to redeem mankind by love. This does not mean simply applying formulas that were good in the 13th Century—though these are not necessarily out of place either. But we must discover new solutions for problems that are entirely new in our age. The discovery is not the work of science only, but above all the work of love.

The history of the Church is a confusion of successes and apparent failures of Christianity. It is in fact an ever-repeated series of attempts to begin constructing the Kingdom of God on earth. This is not surprising, nor is it something Christ Himself failed to foresee. The parable of the cockle sown among the wheat shows clearly that He had this in mind, and that it accords with His Father's plan.

The life of the Church in history as well as the life of the individual Christian is a constantly repeated act of starting over again, of good intentions ending in achievements and in mistakes: of errors that have to be set right, of failings that have to be utilized, of lessons that are learned poorly and have to be learned over again. There have been hesitations and false starts in Christian history. There have even been grave errors, but these are imputable to Christian secular societies rather than to the Church. The Church alone has never lost her way. But the thing that keeps her on the right way is not power, not human wisdom, not political dexterity, or diplomatic foresight. There are times in the history of the Church when these things became, for Christian leaders, stones of stumbling and sources of delusion. The thing that keeps the Church and the Christian on the right way is love. And this is necessary, because love is the highest expression of personality and of freedom.

The Kingdom of God is, then, not the Kingdom of those who merely preach a doctrine or follow certain religious practices: it is the Kingdom of those who love. To build the Kingdom of God is to build a society that is based entirely on freedom and love. It is to build a society which is founded on respect for the individual person, since only persons are capable of love.

One cannot help getting the impression that this is not sufficiently well understood in our day. Love is a word that has been emptied of content by our materialistic society. In our world "love" is reduced to the infatuation celebrated in popular songs. Genuine love cannot be taken for granted, and least of all today. But we Christians seem to take it for granted. We seem to feel that we "love one another" and that we know very well what love is. We tend to act as if things were so well regulated by love in our own household that we could safely forget about it and go out to preach to others. Hence we are not worried about love, so much as about doctrine. At all costs we want to get everybody to agree with us, and to accept our beliefs.

In this way we tend to become proselytizers rather than apostles. That is to say that we are looking for "members" who, by their numbers and their material support will bolster up our own faith and give us more confidence in the doctrine that we preach.

The true Apostle is not preaching a doctrine or leading a movement or recruiting for an organization: he is preaching Christ, because he loves other men and knows that thus he can bring them happiness, and give meaning to their lives. The proselytizer is selling his doctrine because he needs proselytes. The Apostle is preaching Christ because men need the mercy of God and because only in the love of Christ can they find happiness. The proselytizer is bitter and impatient when his ambitions are thwarted: and when they are successful he only communicates his own bitterness and restlessness to those whom he has "converted" into a replica of himself. The Apostle has no ambitions for himself, and his faith is so deep that it does not depend on being preached with great exterior success: even if no one were to believe him, the Apostle would continue quietly and patiently to preach the love of God for man in Christ, without hackneyed slogans, without arrogance and without the salesman's insufferable insistence.

The spirit of proselytism grows out of human cupidity and ambition, and it is this which endangers the purity of the Christian faith in our age, by making Christianity sometimes too like the mass movements that are springing up everywhere. For proselytism, not being "rooted and grounded in charity" (Ephesians 3:17) but springing rather from a hidden anxiety for domination and power, is overanxious to imitate the techniques and the policies of politicians and business men.

It is quite true that the Church must make use of the great new inventions of our age in order to preach the Gospel far and wide. But the Christian apostle must learn how to use these things in a different spirit and with different techniques from the man of the world. The radio and newspaper publicity that surrounds for example the death of a Pope, his burial, and the election and coronation of his successor, can immensely debase the dignity and significance of the Church's symbolic rituals by presenting them in the senseless clichés of journalese.

Christianity loses its meaning when it is described in the language of those whose mind is a constant series of uninterpreted sensations. Filtered through this tepid medium and reduced to the same formless neutrality that emasculates every other truth as soon as it becomes "news," the realities of Christianity and the Church have nothing whatever to gain and everything to lose by mere "publicity." Unless we strive to develop a greater spirit of self-criticism and discretion in our use of the mass-media that have been developed by business and politics, we run a serious risk of becoming, in spite of ourselves, a "party" of parades, slogans and mass demonstrations.

There *must* of course be huge concourses of the faithful in witness of the glories of our faith, but no matter how large a congregation of Christians may be, if it is fully Christian it is never merely a crowd, never merely a mass meeting. The individual is always more important than the collectivity. This is manifested in a rather striking way by the cures that take place, at times, during great demonstrations at Lourdes. The important thing is not that there is a huge crowd singing or praying, but that *one person* who was crippled gets up and goes away whole. The joy of all is simply the amplification of the joy of that one.

It is deeply significant that in any gathering of Christians, each individual person present is so important that a spiritual or temporal favor granted to him can burst into a thousandfold increase of joy in the whole multitude praising God.

A mass-movement is a pyramid at whose summit a few powerful men thrive and grow stronger on the labors of the huge anonymous mass which sacrifices itself in adoration of them. The Kingdom of God is just the opposite: it is the Kingdom of One who being equal to God took the form of a servant and suffered the death of the Cross that the love and life of God might descend and reach out into the lowest depths and bring light to all who are sitting in darkness, poverty, hopelessness and the shadow of death. In the Kingdom of God those who are higher exist for those who are below them. As Christ said:

> The princes of the gentiles lord it over them and they that are greater exercise power upon them. It shall not be so among you: but whosoever will be the greater among you, let him be your minister, and he that will be first among you shall be your servant.

(Matt. 20:25-27)

No matter how gigantic the Christian congregation may sometimes become in its zeal to bear massive witness to its faith in Christ, the type of the Christian gathering will always remain not the parade of thousands of loyal members of a "cause" but the family of the faithful reunited peacefully for the breaking of Bread in the Holy Eucharist, the Lord's Supper. The supreme manifestation of Christian unity is always the relatively small group that gathers around the altar for Mass. The Holy Sacrifice is indeed magnificently impressive when it is offered before an enormous multitude in a stadium, at a Eucharistic congress. Yet it is far more truly itself when it simply unites the members of a parish in the parish Church early on a Sunday morning. By way of analogy, the daily meal which unites families and friends together in the evening, at home, is much more truly significant and human in its ordinariness and genuine warmth than the elaborate formal banquet where a hundred strangers get together in a hotel to nibble at strange cooking and listen to a series of speeches.

Karl Marx's basic charge against religion was that it engineered a systematic *alienation* of the human spirit. It took man away from himself, and from his own spirit. It emptied his life of its personal content to make him a "thing" belonging to something and someone else. It reduced him from the status of an individual person living his own life and forging his own future, to that of a "believer," an anonymous cipher in a religious organization, a worshipper of invisible powers, who devotes his energies and his income to the service of a fiction which he himself creates: a fiction whose existence is encouraged and abetted by the economic rulers of his world.

There is no doubt a certain crudity in Marx's conception. It represents an analysis of religion *from the outside*, by one whose religious instincts had remained frustrated. Marx was not a man without religion: he was a man whose religious development had been thwarted by the practical bourgeois indifferentism and hypocrisy in the midst of which he lived. But his hidden religious energies certainly found a devious outlet in the obvious messianism of his philosophy. In any case, his idea of man's alienation by religion, economics, politics and philosophy is his most genial contribution to the history of human thought. There is no need for Christianity to fear this sharp instrument of Marxian criticism. It becomes indeed one of our own most potent weapons if we turn it against those who claim to be the inheritors of Marx's thought.

Where has man's spirit ever reached such a pitch of alienation as in the mass movements of the twentieth century, and especially in the Soviet Union? The intellectual, spiritual, artistic and religious life of the Soviet citizen has been systematically drained at its source by communist indoctrination. The pseudo-scientific "organization" of man's life in all its departments, not for his benefit but for the benefit of the "revolution" (that is for the heads of the communist Party) has completely emptied man's life of personal

meaning and enterprise. The present disturbances and reactions among Russian youth (hooliganism and stilyagism),
bear eloquent witness to the sense of futility aroused by this
emptying and de-personalization of man's life. The most
ironical fact about the twentieth century is that Atheistic
Communism has finally realized, in its ultimate perfection,
the economic alienation of man which Karl Marx ascribed
in part to religion.

We may be tempted, for a moment, to smile at this
strange confirmation of all that our faith teaches us of the
ways of God with man—that the most effective way in
which man is "punished" on this earth is to let his errors
take their course and work themselves out to their logical
conclusion. Yet we are in no position to sit back and enjoy
a complacent triumph. These same errors are all too likely
to be our own.

We are living in an age of universal alienation and mass
movements. Christian circles are by no means immune from
the contagion of totalitarianism. It is all too easy for us to
seek a kind of massive, monolithic strength in discipline,
publicity, and proselytism. It is all too easy for us to lose
sight of Christ and His charity, and to exchange the basic
truths of the Gospel for new slogans that promise to be
"more effective" in rallying thousands to our cause. Let us
beware. The blaring of loudspeakers, the roaring of slogans,
the tramp of marching thousands, will never produce anything but alienated fanatics. Christianity can never be allowed to savor of a mass-movement. Christians can never,
with a good conscience, yield to the lure of totalitarianism.
Even when a political system promises a strong arm with
which to defend the Church, if that arm ends in a mailed
fist, and if the "protection" offered is that of a secret police
and concentration camps, we cannot accept its protection.

If that system offers to "defend the faith" by the atomic bombing of defenseless civilians, we cannot accept its protection. Such defense is a mockery and a desecration of God in His image. It is a renewal of the crucifixion of Christ, in those for whom He died.

Our mission in the world is the same as it has always been, to build the Kingdom of God, which is a Kingdom of Love. Love cannot exist except between persons. For there to be love, we must first of all safeguard the liberty and integrity of the human person. We must provide an education that strengthens man against the noise, the violence, the slogans and the half-truths of our materialistic society.

Our duty to preserve the human person in his integrity, his freedom and his individuality, and to arm him spiritually against the peril of totalitarianism, is not just something it would be nice for us to discuss and perhaps to study. It is an urgent task which demands insistently to be carried out wherever there is a Catholic parish, a Catholic school, and especially a Catholic university or seminary. It is the most important duty of the Catholic intellectual. It is not an easy task. It is a very delicate one, precisely because our zeal against one type of mass-movement can so easily plunge us head first into another and worse kind of which we are less afraid.

The experience of the past ten years has shown, or should have shown, that it is not enough to be anti-communist to preserve freedom in America. What will the next ten years bring? There is unfortunately all too great a danger that it will see the rise of a fatal mass movement for which the moral and cultural disorder of twentieth-century America have prepared the way only too well.